The Complete Relationship Guide for Couples

The Ultimate Workbook to Deepen Understanding, Enhance Communication, Build and Restore Trust, Increase Intimacy, and Strengthen Your Bond

Riley Andrews

Copyright © 2024 by Riley Andrews

All rights reserved. No part of this publication may be reproduced, stored or transmitted in any form or by any means, electronic, mechanical, photocopying, recording, scanning, or otherwise without written permission from the publisher. It is illegal to copy this book, post it to a website, or distribute it by any other means without permission.

Riley Andrews asserts the moral right to be identified as the author of this work.

Riley Andrews has no responsibility for the persistence or accuracy of URLs for external or third-party Internet Websites referred to in this publication and does not guarantee that any content on such Websites is, or will remain, accurate or appropriate.

Designations used by companies to distinguish their products are often claimed as trademarks. All brand names and product names used in this book and on its cover are trade names, service marks, trademarks and registered trademarks of their respective owners. The publishers and the book are not associated with any product or vendor mentioned in this book. None of the companies referenced within the book have endorsed the book.

First edition

Table of Contents

Introduction	5
1. Active Listening	9
2. Navigating the Terrain of Needs and Desires	19
3. Unraveling the Knots of Conflict	29
4. Nurturing Harmony Through Conflict	41
5. The Alchemy of Emotional Intimacy	53
6. Fostering Physical Connection and Intimacy	67
7. Integrating Financial Unity into the Fabric of Love	79
8. Cultivating and Safeguarding Connection Amidst Life's Transformations	89
9. Exploring the Impact of Betrayal: Steps Toward Healing	101
10. Navigating the Tides of Jealousy and Insecurity	113
11. Cultivating Mutual Respect and Appreciation	125
12. Planning Together for the Adventure of Tomorrow	133
Conclusion	145
Chapter References	151

Introduction

Welcome to a journey that promises to transform your relationship and redefine how you view love, partnership, and mutual growth. Understanding, communication, trust, intimacy, and development are at the heart of every enduring relationship—not lofty ideals but tangible, achievable realities. This book is your pathway to turning these ideas into the foundation of your relationship.

My passion for the power of love and partnership to overcome obstacles is deep-seated and personal. I've witnessed—and lived—the transformative effect that practical, actionable strategies can have on relationships. Drawing from a rich tapestry of experiences and observations, I am thrilled to share insights that I believe can turn any relationship around, making it survive and thrive.

This is not your average relationship guide. "The Complete Relationship Guide for Couples" is a meticulously crafted workbook that embraces inclusivity across all stages of relationships. It's been designed with a keen awareness of the diverse financial realities couples face, ensuring that the exercises and activities are adaptable and relevant to everyone. This unique approach combines comprehensive expert advice with practical, real-world exercises, making it a standout resource for couples everywhere.

The vision behind this workbook is clear: to offer an indispensable tool that tackles joint relationship pain points head-on. By reflecting on their roots and providing adaptable exercises, the workbook is designed to enrich relationships, fostering understanding, trust, and intimacy. It draws on the wisdom of renowned researchers, psychologists, and therapists, integrating their insights with practical exercises. This ensures that the knowledge contained within these pages is credible and actionable.

What sets this workbook apart is its universality and inclusivity. Designed for all couples—regardless of gender, age, sexual orientation, or relationship stage—its exercises are crafted to be adaptable and relevant, making no assumptions about your financial situation. It's filled with activities you can start using immediately, based on solid research and real-world applicability, ensuring you can see tangible improvements in your relationship.

Let me share a brief story from my own life. Several years ago, I found myself at a crossroads in my relationship, struggling with communication and feeling disconnected. We were talking, but "at" each other, not "with" each other. We were spending all our time focusing "in" the relationship and not working "on" the relationship. Only when we committed to actively working on our relationship—using exercises similar to those in this book—did we see a profound change. This personal journey of learning and growth in relationships is what motivates me to share this workbook with you.

As you turn these pages, you'll discover a structured path that focuses on understanding your partner, improving communication, building or recovering trust, enhancing intimacy, and growing together. This roadmap is designed to guide you through the transformative journey ahead, filled with hope and promise for a deeper connection as a couple.

I invite you to dive into this workbook with an open heart and mind, ready to explore the practical exercises and insights within. This workbook is for couples, not individuals. You have to work on this together. The level of commitment to the process will determine the level of growth and development you and your partner will experience. Let's embark on this transformative journey towards a stronger, more understanding, and evolving union.

How You Should Use This Book

This guide is meticulously designed to empower couples to fortify and enrich every facet of their partnership. It is segmented into chapters that each address a pivotal aspect of relationships: Conflict, Intimacy, Financial Dynamics, Navigating Life Changes, Fostering and Restoring Trust, Overcoming Jealousy and Insecurity, Cultivating Respect and Appreciation, and Pursuing Shared Goals and Aspirations. Delving into these areas, the book presents a range of activities and exercises tailored for completion individually and as a couple, aimed at fostering growth and strengthening bonds. Should a particular issue demand immediate attention, readers are encouraged to engage directly with the relevant chapter. Nevertheless, it is recommended to begin with the initial two chapters, which serve as the cornerstone for relationship growth, focusing on the art of listening and the expression of needs and desires. These initial sections offer detailed guidance and practical exercises designed to establish a strong foundation for communication, setting the stage for successful interaction in subsequent chapters. By establishing a fundamental understanding of effective listening and communication—characterized by love, care, empathy, and transparency—couples can create a nurturing environment for their relationship to thrive. This approach ensures that the insights gained from each chapter take root and flourish, contributing to a vibrant and resilient partnership.

Ultimately, this guide is designed for continual reference, not just a single read-through. I envision it as a valuable tool that you can turn to time and again, particularly when you encounter challenges or obstacles. Revisiting its lessons and exercises should reignite a sense of serenity, solidarity, and connection, reminiscent of the love and dedication that initially propelled you and your partner to embark on this path.

Active Listening

In many relationships, truly listening to one's partner often becomes overshadowed by the hustle of daily life, the distractions of the digital age, and the cacophony of our thoughts and preoccupations. Yet, the seeds of understanding and intimacy are sown in the quiet, focused attention to our partner's words. While simple in explanation, the concept of active listening is profound in its impact on relationships. It's a skill that, when honed, has the power to transform the dynamics of interactions, fostering a deeper connection and understanding between partners.

Understanding Active Listening

Active listening is a method of listening that involves giving full attention to the speaker, understanding their message, responding thoughtfully, and retaining the information shared. It's a step beyond the passive absorption of words, requiring the listener to engage fully with the speaker's message. This form of listening is not innate; it's a skill that necessitates intention and practice to develop fully.

The distinction between active listening and passive hearing lies in the engagement level of the listener. While passive hearing is a default mode, where the listener may hear the words but not fully process or engage with the content, active listening demands the listener's complete focus and participation. It's the difference between hearing the melody of a song in the background and intently listening to the lyrics, understanding the story or message being conveyed. In relationships, this distinction becomes crucial. Passive hearing can often lead to misunderstandings or feelings of being undervalued, as it may seem that the listener is disinterested or dismissive of the speaker's emotions or needs.

To engage in active listening, one must employ several key components: paraphrasing, reflecting, and questioning for clarity. Paraphrasing involves repeating what the speaker has said in the listener's own words, demonstrating understanding, and allowing for any miscommunications to be corrected promptly. Conversely, reflecting is about mirroring the emotions or underlying sentiments expressed by the speaker, showing empathy and validation. Questioning for clarity is crucial; it involves asking open-ended questions to delve deeper into the speaker's message, ensuring that the listener fully comprehends the depth and breadth of what is being communicated.

Mastering active listening within a relationship has manifold benefits. At its core, active listening serves as a bridge to deeper empathy and understanding between partners. It allows for the accurate transmission of thoughts and emotions, reducing the likelihood of misunderstandings that can lead to conflict. Furthermore, when one feels truly heard and understood, it fosters a sense of emotional safety and intimacy, strengthening the bond between partners. This emotional safety net becomes the foundation for building trust and a deeper connection.

Consider a scenario where one partner comes home from work, visibly upset about a challenging day. Instead of offering solutions or dismissing the feelings expressed, the other partner engages in active listening. They paraphrase the concerns ("So, it sounds like you felt overlooked during the meeting today"), reflect on the emotions ("That must have been really frustrating"), and ask questions to understand better ("What do you think would have made it better?"). This approach validates the first partner's feelings and opens up a space for meaningful conversation and emotional connection.

In practice, active listening can transform the simplest interactions into moments of connection and understanding. It's about making a conscious decision to be present with your partner, hear them truly, and fully engage with their thoughts and emotions. This doesn't mean that every conversation requires such depth of focus, but in moments of emotional significance, active listening can be the key to unlocking a deeper understanding and intimacy.

Active listening is not merely a tool for navigating the complexities of a relationship; it's a gesture of respect and love. It signals to your partner that you value their thoughts, feelings, and experiences. By dedicating your full attention and effort to understanding them, you're nurturing the emotional connection that is the lifeblood of your relationship. As such, active listening is not just about the words spoken or heard; it's about the space created between partners—a space of mutual respect, understanding, and deep connection.

Barriers to Listening and How to Overcome Them

Communication shapes our most intimate relationships. The flow of that communication can be frequently interrupted by obstacles that hinder our capacity to listen attentively. These barriers, ranging from preconceived notions to the buzz of a smartphone, can distort or drown out the message our partner is trying to convey, leading to misinterpretation and conflict. Recognizing and dismantling these obstacles is crucial in fostering a climate of understanding and empathy within our relationships.

Preconceptions can be a significant barrier to active listening, coloring our perception of our partner's words with our biases and experiences. This distortion filter can lead to misinterpretation, as we might hear what we expect to hear rather than what is actually being said. The antidote to this cognitive distortion is approaching conversations with an open mind, consciously setting aside our judgments and assumptions. This requires a degree of self-awareness, a willingness to challenge our own perceptions, and the humility to accept that our understanding may not always align with reality.

Distractions, both external and internal, further complicate the listening process. The external ones are often easier to identify: the ping of a notification, the television in the background, or the bustle of a crowded room. These can usually be managed by creating a conducive environment for conversation, such as turning off electronics, choosing a quiet space, or simply facing each other to signify that your full attention is on the dialogue. Nothing says, "You are important to me" more than turning off your phone, tablet, or television and looking at your partner. Internal distractions, however, are more insidious. Our thoughts, worries, and preoccupations can pull our focus away from the conversation, leading to a half-hearted engagement where we're physically present but mentally elsewhere. Addressing these requires a conscious effort to clear our minds before engaging in a conversation, perhaps through a brief moment of meditation or simply taking a few deep breaths to center ourselves.

Emotional reactions often serve as both a barrier and a catalyst to miscommunication. Intense feelings, whether they are anger, sadness, or even excitement, can cloud our ability to listen objectively. In moments of high emotion, our instinct might be to defend, argue, or shut down, none of which are conducive to productive conversation. The key to managing these reactions lies in recognizing the signs of escalating emotion within ourselves and employing strategies to moderate these feelings. This might involve pausing the conversation to allow for a cooling-off period or using calming techniques such as deep breathing or visualization to regain our composure. Maintaining control over our emotional responses creates space for empathy and understanding to flourish.

Mindfulness practices offer a powerful tool for overcoming the barriers to effective listening. By cultivating a state of present-moment awareness, we learn to focus our attention fully on our partner, tuning out distractions and quieting our internal monologue. This heightened state of awareness not only improves our ability to listen but also enriches our empathetic engagement with our partner's emotional landscape. Practicing mindfulness can be as simple as engaging in regular meditation sessions, which train the mind to focus and refocus attention, or it can be integrated into daily activities such as eating, walking, or even listening to music, with an emphasis on fully experiencing the present moment without judgment. Mindfulness can be practiced in even simple activities, such as drying your hands. Slow down. Focus on the texture of the towel. Feel it drying the palm of each hand and then focus on drying each finger individually. These seconds of recentering yourself help build a continuity of mindfulness throughout your day and life.

The act of listening extends beyond the mere processing of words. It involves an intricate blend of attention, empathy, and self-regulation, all of which are susceptible to the disruptions caused by barriers such as preconceptions, distractions, emotional reactions, and a lack of mindfulness. Overcoming these barriers requires not just awareness but a commitment to continuous practice and self-improvement. Through this process, we enhance our ability to listen and deepen our connections, fostering a relationship grounded in mutual understanding and respect.

Exercises to Enhance Listening Skills

Active listening forms the cornerstone of deep, meaningful connections in intimate relationships, creating a foundation of understanding and empathy that bolsters the partnership. This collection of exercises, each unique but complementary, offers a hands-on approach to cultivating these crucial skills.

Mirroring Exercise

At the heart of the mirroring exercise lies the simple yet profound act of echoing your partner's words, a method that validates their experience and fosters a deeper mutual understanding. Initiate this practice in moments of tranquility, where distractions are minimized, and the focus can fully rest on the exchange. One partner begins by sharing a thought or feeling, encapsulating a moment or emotion they wish to convey. The listening partner, with intent and care, mirrors this message, not as a parrot but with genuine comprehension and empathy. This reflection is then validated by the original speaker, ensuring the essence of their message was accurately captured. Through this iterative process, nuances of communication are refined, misunderstandings are clarified, and a profound sense of being heard and understood is cultivated.

Active Listening Role Play

The dynamics of active listening role play introduce a layer of complexity and learning, simulating real-life scenarios within a controlled environment to sharpen listening skills. This exercise calls for partners to craft scenarios reflecting common communication challenges, ranging from mundane misunderstandings to deeper emotional disclosures. Each partner takes turns in both the speaker and listener roles, navigating the scenario with the active listening strategies they've been cultivating. This role reversal is instrumental, offering each person a dual perspective: as a listener, to hone their empathetic listening and response skills, and as a speaker, to appreciate the effort and attentiveness required in active listening. Through this empathetic role exchange, insights into the other's emotional world are gained, and the practice of active listening is solidified.

Daily Listening Time

Establishing a daily ritual dedicated to uninterrupted listening offers a consistent framework for nurturing active listening skills. This simple practice involves setting aside a designated time each day where partners commit to sharing and listening without distractions. This time becomes a sacred space for open, honest communication, where each partner takes turns speaking, ensuring both voices are heard equally. During these sessions, the listener's role is not to offer solutions or judgments but to offer their undivided attention, validating and reflecting the speaker's thoughts and feelings. This daily commitment acts as a reinforcing mechanism, gradually embedding active listening into the fabric of the relationship, transforming it into a natural, automatic response. The beginning doesn't have to be long to be effective. The key is to commit to the time and show up for your partner. Start with just a few minutes and increase the time as you both choose. Begin simply. Don't try to explore the emotional conflict points on the first day. Create the practice and let it grow into a safe place for both you and your partner to share thoughts, feelings, and worries. There is no wrong way to do this except not to do it.

Feedback Loop

The integration of a feedback loop into the practice of active listening serves as a critical tool for continual improvement and adjustment. After engaging in any of the aforementioned exercises, partners are encouraged to share feedback on their listening experience, highlighting areas of strength and opportunities for growth. This feedback, delivered with kindness and constructive intent, is invaluable, providing insights into how each partner perceives and processes the act of being listened to. It's through this open exchange of feedback that misunderstandings can be preemptively addressed, and active listening skills are finely tuned. Moreover, this loop fosters an environment of mutual learning and adaptation, where the act of listening evolves in harmony with the relationship's dynamics.

In the pursuit of enhancing listening skills within intimate relationships, these exercises serve as practical, actionable steps. Each exercise, from mirroring to the establishment of a feedback loop, offers a unique avenue for growth, understanding, and connection. Through regular, committed practice, the art of active listening transcends the realm of exercise, becoming an integral thread in the tapestry of the relationship, enriching communication and deepening the bond between partners.

Listening Beyond Words: The Role of Body Language

Body language, composed of subtle gestures, shifts in posture, and the flicker of expressions across our faces, often conveys more than our words ever could. Attuning to this undercurrent of communication requires a nuanced awareness and sensitivity to the unspoken feelings and thoughts that our partners express not with words but with the very movement and stillness of their being.

The significance of body language, tone, and facial expressions in the realm of communication cannot be overstated. These non-verbal cues act as amplifiers of our verbal messages, imbuing them with emotion and intent. They can affirm or contradict the words we speak, offering a deeper insight into our genuine feelings. For instance, the warmth in our tone can soften a difficult message, while a tense posture might reveal underlying discomfort, even as we speak reassuring words. Recognizing the harmony, or indeed the dissonance, between verbal and non-verbal communication is pivotal in understanding the complete message being conveyed.

Ensuring alignment between our words and body language is an act of authenticity, demonstrating our commitment to transparent and honest communication. This alignment reassures our partner of the sincerity behind our words, fostering a deeper trust. Our messages resonate most profoundly in the congruence of a gentle touch paired with words of love or the consistency of open posture when offering support. Achieving this synchrony might necessitate a heightened self-awareness, an internal calibration of sorts, where we consciously ensure that our non-verbal cues reflect our true intentions and feelings.

Deciphering our partner's non-verbal cues invites us into a deeper communion with their emotional world. Like learning a new language, this skill demands patience and attentiveness. It begins with observation, noticing the nuances of their body language in various contexts and mapping these observations to their expressed feelings and thoughts. Over time, patterns emerge – a certain look that precedes laughter, the tension that signals stress, or the subtle signs of discomfort we might otherwise miss. Recognizing these cues allows us to respond more empathetically, addressing the words and feelings behind them. It's in the silent moments, watching a sunset together or sitting in shared solitude, that these non-verbal dialogues often speak loudest, conveying love, contentment, or concern without a word needing to be spoken.

Non-verbal affirmations, those subtle yet powerful gestures of engagement and empathy, are the currency of deep connection. A nod, a touch, or maintaining eye contact are not mere courtesies but profound affirmations of our presence and participation in the conversation. They signal to our partner that we are fully with them, immersed in the exchange, valuing their words and essence. These gestures of acknowledgment go beyond the mere mechanics of conversation, weaving a stronger bond between us, a thread of connection that transcends the spoken word. They are the silent affirmations of our care, interest, and commitment to the relationship.

Where words and silences swirl in the dance of understanding and connection, body language offers a window into the soul. It reveals the hidden depths of emotion and thought that words alone might mask. Attuning to this silent language, aligning our non-verbal cues with our verbal messages, and reading our partner's non-verbal expressions deepen our empathy and strengthen our bond. It's in these nuances, the subtle gestures, and expressions that the true art of listening lies – listening not just with our ears, eyes, hearts, and very beings.

Navigating the Terrain of Needs and Desires

Identifying and expressing our needs and desires is like plotting a course for a journey together. Without this clear direction, we risk meandering without purpose, becoming ensnared in misunderstandings and the disappointment of unmet needs. By thoughtfully considering what sustains our emotional health and bravely sharing these insights, we chart a course toward a rewarding relationship.

Identifying Your Needs and Desires

Self-Reflection

Understanding our needs begins in the quiet introspection of our desires, away from the clamor of daily obligations. It's a moment of pause, a breath in the continuum of our existence, where we ask ourselves, "What is it that truly nourishes my soul?" This inquiry is not superficial; it demands honesty and vulnerability, peeling back the layers of societal expectations and personal pretenses to reveal the core of our emotional and physical necessities.

Consider a moment when you felt truly content—what elements were present? Was it the warmth of companionship, the satisfaction of achievement, or perhaps the peace of solitude? These instances provide invaluable clues, illuminating the contours of our needs and desires.

Differentiating Needs from Wants

In delineating our needs from our wants, we draw a line in the sand between the essentials for our emotional equilibrium and the desires that, while enriching, are not critical. This distinction is crucial, for it prioritizes our focus, ensuring that our energies are directed toward what is fundamentally necessary for our well-being.

Imagine standing in a garden, deciding between watering a fruit-bearing tree and a beautiful but non-essential flower. Both add value to the garden, yet the tree's yield is vital for sustenance. Similarly, recognizing that communication, respect, and intimacy might be needs, whereas extravagant vacations and grand gestures might be wants, helps align our efforts toward nurturing what truly sustains the relationship.

Prioritizing Needs

Once identified, our needs must be arranged in a hierarchy, understanding that not all needs carry equal weight at all times. This prioritization is fluid, adapting to the changing landscapes of our lives and relationships. It's akin to navigating through a city with a map; while all destinations hold importance, selecting the most pressing route ensures efficiency and satisfaction.

In practical application, envision a scenario where one partner is experiencing a demanding period at work, filled with deadlines and high-stress projects. During such times, the need for calm and supportive companionship may surpass the usual enthusiasm for engaging in adventurous and energetic outings. Recognizing and acknowledging this shift in needs is vital. By openly communicating this change, perhaps saying, "Right now, I find myself needing a quiet evening with you more than a night out," you invite your partner into your current reality. This shared understanding fosters a supportive environment, ensuring that both partners are aligned in navigating this challenging phase together, reinforcing the bond of mutual care and understanding.

Using "I" Statements

The articulation of our needs is a delicate endeavor, requiring language that fosters openness rather than defensiveness. "I" statements are powerful tools in this regard, framing our expressions of need as personal reflections rather than criticisms. Instead of saying, "You never spend time with me," opting for, "I feel valued when we spend quality time together," shifts the focus from blame to an expression of desire, paving the way for constructive dialogue.

This approach is not merely about semantics; it's about creating a space where vulnerability is met with empathy, where the expression of needs strengthens rather than strains the bonds of partnership.

As we navigate through the intricate terrain of our needs and desires, we must be guided by the principles of self-awareness, honesty, and courage to reveal our true selves. This journey of self-discovery and expression lays the groundwork for a fulfilling partnership, leading us toward greater empathy and shared happiness.

Constructive Ways to Express Your Needs

Timing and Setting

The ambiance and moment chosen for the revelation of one's desires and needs significantly impact the reception of these sentiments. Optimal timing serves as a conduit, ensuring the message traverses the distance between partners with clarity and receptivity. In the soft glow of the evening when the day's clamor has subsided, or perhaps during a shared morning ritual, when the mind is unburdened by the day's obligations, words find fertile ground. In these interludes of tranquility, the heart's utterances can be most profoundly heard and understood. Similarly, the setting acts as a silent participant in the conversation, a space devoid of distractions, where intimacy wraps around the duo, fostering an atmosphere of openness and empathy. Whether it is the quietude of a living room couch, under the canopy of stars, or a bench in a secluded corner of a park, the chosen environment subtly influences the depth and authenticity of the exchange.

Effective Communication Strategies

The articulation of needs and desires demands a strategy that bridges the gap between thought and expression, ensuring the essence of our sentiments is not lost in translation. Clarity in language emerges as a beacon, guiding the conversation with precision and avoiding the pitfalls of ambiguity. Words chosen with care and intention illuminate the true nature of our needs, leaving little room for misinterpretation. Concurrently, the eschewal of blame transforms the dialogue, removing barriers and defensiveness and paving the way for constructive engagement. Phrases laden with accusations become replaced with expressions of personal feeling and perspective, shifting the focus from fault-finding to understanding. Moreover, orienting the conversation towards solutions rather than dwelling on the problem encourages a collaborative approach, where both partners engage in a mutual quest for harmony and fulfillment.

Emotional Honesty

The act of baring one's soul, revealing the raw, unfiltered essence of our emotional landscape, is an endeavor marked by courage and vulnerability. This emotional honesty is the cornerstone of meaningful dialogue, where the revelation of our true feelings becomes the bridge to deeper connection. In acknowledging our fears, hopes, and desires without the armor of pretense, we invite our partner into the sanctum of our inner world. This openness fosters a climate of trust and humanizes our needs, rendering them tangible and relatable. It is a testament to strength, not a sign of weakness, revealing the depth of our commitment to the relationship and the pursuit of mutual understanding. In stripping away the facades, we lay the foundation for a dialogue rooted in authenticity, where vulnerability becomes the very thread that weaves the fabric of closeness and intimacy.

Request vs. Demand

In open and honest communication, the distinction between making a request and issuing a demand becomes paramount. Requests imbued with flexibility and respect for the other's autonomy, invite collaboration. They are expressions of desire that leave room for negotiation, acknowledging the partner's capacity for choice and agency. Demands, however, stand in stark contrast, marked by rigidity and an expectation of compliance. They create an atmosphere of coercion, where the balance of power is skewed, and the dignity of choice is overshadowed by the weight of obligation. Learning to frame our needs as requests is an art that necessitates mindfulness and empathy. It involves the careful selection of words and an awareness of tone and body language, ensuring that the spirit of partnership and mutual respect is preserved. This nuanced approach shifts from a singular focus on fulfillment to a broader vision of reciprocal understanding and cooperation.

Expressing our needs and desires is challenging. We engage in a process that is both introspective and interpersonal. The choice of timing and setting, the clarity and constructiveness of our communication, the authenticity of our emotional expression, and the framing of our needs as requests rather than demands coalesce to form a dialogue that enriches and deepens our relationships. Through this thoughtful engagement, we find not only the expression of our innermost selves but also the path to mutual understanding and fulfillment.

Navigating Your Partner's Defensive Responses

Understanding Defensive Responses

When vulnerability intertwines with open communication, vulnerability can sometimes hang up on defensiveness. These reactions are not anomalies but rather deeply human responses to perceived threats. At their core, they represent a shield raised against potential harm—be it to one's ego, sense of self, or emotional security. Recognizing this allows for an approach marked not by frustration but by empathy. To understand defensive responses, one must look beneath the surface reaction, acknowledging the underlying fears and insecurities that fuel them. It is akin to navigating a labyrinth; patience and a keen sense of direction are essential. Therefore, a partner's defensive posture is not an impasse but an invitation to explore deeper, to engage with the underlying vulnerabilities and insecurities that lie at the heart of their reaction.

De-escalation Techniques

In moments where the air between partners becomes charged with the electricity of rising defensiveness, de-escalation becomes the grounding wire. Techniques to diffuse tension are numerous, yet they converge on the principle of reducing emotional volatility to foster a climate conducive to understanding. One effective strategy is the intentional lowering of one's voice, a subtle cue that invites calm and signals no threat. Similarly, adopting open body language—uncrossed arms, relaxed posture—acts as a non-verbal reassurance, a physical manifestation of openness to dialogue. Pausing before responding, allowing a breath or two to pass, creates a buffer against reactive responses, granting both parties space to collect their thoughts and emotions. When employed with mindfulness, these techniques act as a balm on the heated skin of a conversation, soothing tempers and paving the way for constructive engagement.

Reassurance and Support

In the shadow of defensiveness, reassurance acts as a beacon, guiding the conversation back to a place of safety and mutual respect. It is an affirmation that, even in the midst of disagreement or misunderstanding, the foundation of the relationship—its bonds of affection and respect—remains unshaken. Offering reassurance is an act of nurturing, verbal and non-verbal communication that expressing needs is not an indictment but a step towards shared happiness. This can take the form of affirming statements acknowledging the validity of a partner's feelings while gently redirecting focus toward resolution. "I hear your concerns and they are valid. My intention is not to criticize but to find a way we can both feel fulfilled," serves as a bridge over troubled waters, reaffirming commitment to the relationship and to finding a path forward together.

Finding Common Ground

In the quest for compromise, common ground is the terra firma on which both partners can stand together. Discovering this shared space often requires a shift in perspective and a willingness to see beyond individual positions to the overarching goals that unite. This process is akin to piecing together a mosaic, where each compromise is a fragment contributing to creating a shared vision. Techniques to facilitate this include focusing on shared values and long-term objectives, which can often be obscured by the immediacy of conflicting needs. Additionally, engaging in collaborative problem-solving exercises can illuminate areas of agreement that were previously overshadowed by discord. By emphasizing cooperation over contention, finding common ground becomes a means to resolve the current disagreement and a strategy for strengthening the relationship against future challenges.

In the delicate give and take of communication, the path through defensive reactions is navigated with empathy, patience, and a deep commitment to mutual understanding. Through de-escalation, reassurance, and the pursuit of common ground, partners can transcend the immediate friction of conflicting needs, forging a deeper connection rooted in mutual respect and shared goals. This journey through defensiveness to understanding is not linear; it is marked by ebbs and flows, challenges, and triumphs. Yet, within this complexity, the true strength of a relationship is forged, in the willingness to engage, understand, and grow together.

Balancing Needs: Yours, Mine, and Ours

In relationships, strands of individual desires intertwine with shared aspirations, creating a complex whole that demands careful attention to maintain its beauty and strength. The balance between personal needs and mutual objectives is not static but a dynamic equilibrium that requires constant nurturing. This delicate balance is the linchpin of enduring partnerships, ensuring that both individuals flourish without overshadowing the collective harmony of their union.

Navigating the complex terrain of negotiation and compromise requires a thoughtful mix of empathy, understanding, and creativity. Strategies for reaching amicable agreements start with acknowledging the legitimacy of each partner's needs. This recognition forms the bedrock of constructive dialogue, fostering an environment where solutions are not zero-sum games but opportunities for mutual enrichment. Creative problem-solving emerges as a vital tool in this context, encouraging partners to think beyond conventional compromises toward innovative solutions that might fulfill both sets of needs in unanticipated ways. The process is similar to sculpting a block of marble; with each thoughtful negotiation, the relationship's true form, which incorporates both partners' desires and dreams, is gradually revealed.

Amidst the interplay of compromise and cooperation, the preservation of individuality within the relationship stands as a testament to its health and vitality. The essence of each person should not only be preserved but celebrated, for each partner's unique qualities enrich the relationship. Encouraging and supporting personal growth and individual pursuits is akin to tending to the garden of the relationship, ensuring that each flower blooms in its own time and space, adding to the collective beauty. This respect for personal development fosters a deeper sense of fulfillment and contentment, reducing the likelihood of resentment and enhancing the bond shared.

As chapters in the story of a relationship unfold, the narrative weaves through moments of harmony and discord, each phase imbued with lessons and growth. The balance between personal needs and shared goals, the art of negotiation and compromise, the celebration of individuality, and the importance of regular check-ins emerge as pivotal themes in this ongoing saga. These practices are not endpoints but waypoints, markers of a relationship's depth and resilience.

We are reminded that the essence of the partnership lies not in the erasure of the self for the sake of the union but in the harmonious integration of two wholes, creating a synergy that is greater than the sum of its parts. This dance of balance, negotiation, and growth is an ongoing dialogue, a testament to love's living, breathing nature. In the confluence of our shared and individual journeys, it is here that the true beauty of partnership is revealed, not as a destination but as a path we walk together, hand in hand.

As we turn the page, let us carry forward the lessons of balance, empathy, and growth, weaving them into the fabric of our relationships. These principles, illuminated in the discussions that follow, serve as guideposts, illuminating the path toward deeper connection and understanding.

Unraveling the Knots of Conflict

Conflict is an inevitable thread in human connections, its colors as varied as the emotions and circumstances that weave through our relationships. Yet, within these knots of discord lie hidden opportunities for growth, understanding, and deeper intimacy. It is not the presence of conflict that defines the strength of a bond but the manner in which it is navigated. This chapter delves into the common sources that often lead to these clashes, providing insights and strategies not just to untangle them but to transform these moments into catalysts for unity.

Common Sources of Conflict in Relationships

Differences in Values and Beliefs

Individual values and beliefs create a harmony within relationships that is both complex and dynamic. Yet, when these core principles diverge too greatly or clash, the resulting dissonance can lead to profound conflict. Understanding and respecting these differences is paramount; it involves recognizing that the diversity of our backgrounds and experiences shapes our worldview. In a scenario where one partner values independence highly, viewing it as a sign of strength and self-reliance, tensions can arise while the other places a premium on interdependence and collective decision-making. Here, the conflict is not about right or wrong but about finding a balance that honors both perspectives. Strategies such as creating a shared set of values that incorporate the most important aspects of each partner's beliefs can bridge divergent views, fostering a sense of mutual respect and understanding.

Communication Breakdowns

The channels through which we express our thoughts, desires, and frustrations are often fraught with obstacles. Miscommunication, whether through misinterpreted words, mismatched non-verbal signals, or simply the failure to convey one's meaning clearly, is a potent catalyst for conflict. Consider the simple act of planning a weekend getaway, where one partner's suggestion of "Let's go camping" is met with the other's silent reservation, rooted in a preference for comfort over adventure. Without clear communication, this scenario can quickly escalate from a difference in preference to a full-blown argument, underscoring the pivotal role of effective dialogue in preventing misunderstandings.

Unmet Expectations

Expectations, often unspoken, act as silent architects of our relational landscape. When these anticipations—whether they involve daily chores, financial responsibilities, or emotional support—are not met, the foundation of trust and satisfaction can erode. This erosion is akin to the slow, often imperceptible, wear of water on stone, where the initial signs of damage may be overlooked until the structure is compromised. Addressing this source of conflict requires bringing these expectations into the light, discussing them openly, and adjusting them to align more closely with reality and mutual capability.

Stress and External Pressures

External forces, from the demands of work to the dynamics of extended family, exert a considerable influence on the equilibrium of a relationship. When brought into a partnership's shared space, stress can act as a magnifier of existing tensions, transforming minor irritations into major conflicts. A relatable example is the strain financial difficulties place on a relationship, where the pressure to maintain stability becomes a source of constant tension. Recognizing the impact of these external pressures entails acknowledging their presence an actively working together to mitigate their effects, whether through shared problem-solving strategies, support systems, or stress-relief practices.

In dissecting the common sources of conflict within relationships, this chapter lays bare the complexities and challenges that partners face. Yet, it also illuminates the pathways to resolution, understanding, and ultimately, stronger bonds. By acknowledging and addressing differences in values and beliefs, refining communication, managing expectations, and mitigating the impact of external pressures, couples can transform conflict from a source of division to an opportunity for growth.

The Role of Past Experiences in Present Conflicts

Emotional Baggage

Past traumas and experiences subtly influence our behaviors and decisions in the complex network of human relationships, often without our conscious awareness. These remnants of yesteryears, the emotional baggage we carry, serve as unseen forces, guiding our defensive mechanisms in times of conflict. Understanding this phenomenon means recognizing that our past does not merely reside within us as memories but manifests in our present behaviors, particularly in how we navigate disagreements and disputes. The impact of such historical emotional injuries can be profound, instigating a cycle where defensive behavior becomes a reflex, not a choice. This cycle, once initiated, is challenging to break, for it requires not only the acknowledgment of the past's influence but also the willingness to confront and understand these deep-seated fears and vulnerabilities.

Pattern Recognition

Identifying and breaking negative patterns from past experiences is like untangling a knotted thread; it demands patience, persistence, and a keen eye for detail. These patterns, often so ingrained in our behavior that they become second nature, dictate our responses to conflict, leading us down familiar paths of discord and misunderstanding. Recognizing these patterns is the first step toward change. It involves a meticulous process of reflection and analysis, where instances of conflict are dissected to reveal the underlying habits that fuel them. This endeavor is not solitary; it thrives on open dialogue with one's partner, where you map the contours of these recurring cycles together. This understanding makes breaking free from these patterns possible, though not without effort. It requires the deliberate practice of new, constructive behaviors in response to triggers, gradually rewiring the brain's instinctual reactions to conflict.

Projection

The act of projection, wherein one superimposes past hurts and disappointments onto current situations, serves as a lens distorting reality, often escalating conflicts to unforeseen heights. This psychological phenomenon is not merely a relic of our individual histories but a mirror reflecting our deepest insecurities onto our partners. In moments of tension, the mind, in its attempt to protect, might draw parallels between a present disagreement and a past betrayal, intensifying the emotional charge of the interaction. Recognizing when projection is at play is crucial; it demands a high degree of self-awareness and the ability to discern the root of one's emotional responses. Is the intensity of the reaction proportionate to the current issue, or is it magnified by the ghosts of past grievances? This inquiry, though uncomfortable, is essential in disentangling present conflicts from historical emotional entanglements, paving the way for resolutions grounded in the reality of now rather than the echoes of then.

Healing Together

The journey towards healing, particularly in the context of a relationship, is a voyage navigated in tandem. It is a process that transcends the individual, encompassing the collective wounds and histories that each partner brings to the table. This shared path to healing is built on a foundation of mutual acknowledgment and understanding of past pains and how they seep into the fabric of the relationship. Strategies for this collaborative healing process are manifold, yet they converge on the principles of openness, patience, and unconditional support. Initiatives might include joint therapy sessions, where couples explore the caverns of their past experiences guided by a professional, shining a light on the shadows that influence their present. Alternatively, practices such as shared journaling or creating a safe space for regular, open discussions about feelings and fears can foster an environment where healing is not just possible but nurtured. This shared endeavor, while challenging, fortifies the relationship, transforming past adversities into pillars of strength and understanding. Through this collective healing, the specters of past conflicts lose their grip, allowing the relationship to flourish in the richness of the present, unburdened by the weights of yesteryear.

Strategies and Exercises for Uncovering Underlying Issues

Below are four strategies to help uncover underlying issues. The exercises for this chapter are to schedule a time with your partner to practice these strategies. This should be a mutually agreed upon time, where there isn't a conflict with other commitments. This *is* the commitment. During these exercises, don't try to deal with every underlying issue that has ever reared its head in your relationship. Take it slow. Work on a single issue at a time. The goal is not to solve each other's issues, but to see them and to acknowledge them, to validate and accept them. The time for "fixing" each other is never. But it is always the time to understand and love each other.

Open-Ended Questions

Employing open-ended questions in conversations transcends mere dialogue, serving as a beacon that illuminates the terrains of our partner's mind and heart. These inquiries are designed to avoid a simple yes or no response and to encourage a flow of thoughts and feelings, pave a pathway toward deeper understanding. When we pose a question that begins with 'how' or 'what,' we invite our partners to explore the breadth of their emotions, navigate through their thoughts, and arrive at insights that might have remained obscured in the absence of such probing. This method of inquiry does not just open doors to hidden rooms within our partner's psyche; it demonstrates a genuine interest in their inner world, reinforcing the bonds of trust and intimacy that are critical to the sustenance of a relationship. Through this practice, we move beyond the superficial layers of communication, uncovering the intricate and often unvoiced issues and opportunities that lie beneath.

Active Listening in Conflict

When there is conflict, emotions run high, and misunderstandings cloud judgment, the principle of active listening emerges as a linchpin for resolution and understanding. This is not merely about hearing the words spoken by our partner but engaging with them with a depth of focus and empathy that allows for the true essence of their message to permeate our consciousness. It involves deliberately silencing our internal monologue, suspending our judgments and preconceptions, and truly inhabiting the moment with our partner. Through this deep engagement, we can discern the underlying issues that fuel the conflict, issues that might have remained veiled were it not for our committed attentiveness. In this context, active listening is both a gift and a strategy, offering our partner the validation and understanding they seek while equipping us with the insights necessary to navigate through the tumult of discord toward resolution. It is always acceptable to take a time out, de-escalate, and calm down. Uncovering underlying issues can be stressful, and it is wise to take time to process. A time out of no less than 20 minutes gives each partner the opportunity to compose themselves. During this time, do something you enjoy, such as going for a walk or listening to music. The intent is to bring each person back to a balanced emotional state from which to continue dialog.

Emotional Validation

The act of validating our partner's emotions and acknowledging their feelings as both real and significant is a cornerstone in the architecture of healthy communication. Through this acknowledgment, we affirm our partner's right to their emotions, providing a sanctuary for their vulnerabilities and fears. Emotional validation transcends mere agreement, venturing into the realm of empathy where we recognize the validity of our partner's feelings even if we do not share them. This practice is just like offering a hand in the darkness, a gesture that conveys support and understanding even amidst the whirlwind of conflict. It is through this validation that the hidden issues, often cloaked in layers of emotional turbulence, are gently brought into the light, allowing for a dialogue that can address the root causes of discord rather than just its symptoms. By affirming our partner's emotional experiences, we pave the way for a deeper connection and create a climate where underlying issues can be safely explored and addressed.

Using "I Feel" Statements

Framing expressions of emotion with "I feel" statements is a powerful tool in the quest to foster open and blame-free dialogue. This linguistic approach centers on our own experiences and emotions, rather than attributing causality or intent to our partner's actions, thus sidestepping the pitfalls of accusation that can escalate conflicts. When we articulate our feelings with clarity and ownership, we invite our partner into our emotional world, offering them a map of our vulnerabilities without erecting walls of defensiveness. For instance, instead of proclaiming, "You make me feel neglected," opting for, "I feel neglected when we don't spend quality time together," shifts the narrative from blame to personal experience and desire for connection. This method does not merely serve to communicate our emotions more effectively; it also uncovers the deeper layers of our emotional landscape that might be contributing to the conflict. By employing "I feel" statements, we engage in a dialogue that prioritizes understanding and empathy, creating a fertile ground for resolving not only the present conflict but also for nurturing a relationship characterized by deep emotional attunement and respect.

Preventing Escalation: Tips and Techniques

In the area of intimacy in a relationship, the potential for conversations to veer into the territory of heated conflict is ever-present. Recognizing the moments when dialogue threatens to spiral into discord serves as a preventative measure and a testament to the strength and resilience of the connection shared between partners. This recognition hinges on an acute awareness of trigger points, those specific words, tones, or topics that ignite emotional responses. Identifying these trigger points demands a level of introspection and mutual understanding that transcends superficial communication, delving into the subtle dynamics that define the relationship. It involves an ongoing dialogue about emotional landscapes, where partners feel safe expressing their vulnerabilities without fear of judgment. When these trigger points surface in conversation, the ability to pause to acknowledge their presence without allowing them to steer the discourse becomes invaluable. This pause is not a retreat but a strategic recalibration, ensuring that the conversation remains anchored in mutual respect and understanding.

The concept of taking time outs introduces a structured approach to managing moments of heightened emotion, allowing both individuals a breathing space to regain their composure and perspective. Far from evading the issue at hand, this technique offers a necessary interlude, a moment of stillness in which the storm of emotions can subside. The effectiveness of a time out is contingent upon mutual agreement on its purpose and parameters, ensuring that it is not perceived as abandonment but as a shared strategy for conflict resolution. During these time outs, engaging in activities that promote calm and reflection, whether it be a walk in solitude or a few moments of mindful breathing, can significantly alter the emotional tenor of the subsequent conversation. The key lies in the re-engagement post-time out, where both partners return not to resume a battle but to continue a dialogue with renewed clarity and empathy.

The language we wield in moments of conflict holds the power to either escalate or pacify the situation. De-escalation language, characterized by its focus on empathy, validation, and shared understanding, is a balm for frayed nerves and hurt emotions. Phrases that acknowledge the other's feelings ("I understand this is important to you") express a desire for mutual understanding ("Help me understand your perspective") or affirm the value of the relationship ("Our connection is important to me") can significantly defuse potential conflicts. This language, however, must be employed with sincerity; it is not a manipulative tool but a genuine expression of the desire to navigate through discord with grace and mutual respect. The artistry of de-escalation lies not in suppressing disagreement but in transforming conflict into a constructive exploration of differences.

Central to the prevention of escalation is the shift from a mindset of blaming to one of collaborative solution-finding. This shift demands a departure from the quagmire of rigid stances, moving towards the common ground of shared goals and aspirations. It involves framing challenges not as battlegrounds where one must emerge victorious but as puzzles that, when solved together, strengthen the bond between partners. This focus on solutions fosters a sense of teamwork and collaboration, where the energies of both individuals are directed not against each other but toward the resolution of the issue at hand. Techniques such as brainstorming sessions, where both partners contribute ideas without immediate judgment, or the establishment of shared goals that provide a north star for the relationship, can facilitate this shift. The emphasis on solutions acts as a reminder of the ultimate goal of any conflict within a relationship: not to win, but to understand, grow, and deepen the connection shared.

When confronting conflict within intimate relationships, the strategies outlined here serve as navigational aids, guiding couples through the potential minefields of discord toward a landscape of deeper understanding and connection. Recognizing trigger points and employing timeouts offer a framework for managing emotional volatility, while the careful use of de-escalation language and a focus on solutions pave the way for constructive dialogue. Though distinct, these techniques are interconnected threads in the fabric of a resilient relationship, each contributing to creating a partnership characterized by mutual respect, understanding, and growth.

As we draw this exploration to a close, the essence of our discussion coalesces around a central tenet: conflict, inherent to the human experience, holds within it not just the seeds of discord but the potential for profound personal and relational growth. The strategies and insights shared in this chapter are not merely tools for navigating disagreements but steppingstones toward building a relationship that thrives on understanding, empathy, and mutual respect. In the chapters that follow, we continue our journey, delving into the realms of intimacy, trust, and the continual evolution of love.

Nurturing Harmony Through Conflict

Where lives merge, conflict, frequently seen as an unwelcome part of a relationship, can, in fact, foster greater intimacy and comprehension. This realization shifts our perspective, allowing us to view disagreements not as battlegrounds but as arenas for growth. Here, we learn the importance of engaging with conflicts not intending to conquer but to understand, listen, and evolve together.

The art of navigating through disagreements with grace and mutual respect hinges on a set of practices—rules, and boundaries that act as the framework within which healthy conflict can unfold. These practices are not merely theoretical concepts but are deeply rooted in the everyday interactions that define our relationships. They are the silent agreements that guide us, ensuring that even in discord, we remain anchored to respect, understanding, and love.

Steps to Fair Fighting: Rules and Boundaries

Setting Rules for Disagreements

Establishing clear guidelines for how conflicts are approached can change the nature of disagreements from being chaotic and unproductive to becoming structured conversations, where both partners feel heard and respected. Key among these rules is the commitment to refrain from name-calling, a practice that does nothing but inflict hurt and widens the chasm between partners. Equally vital is the agreement not to interrupt, honoring the space for each voice to be heard in its entirety. By focusing solely on the issue at hand, we avoid the trap of digression into irrelevant territories, maintaining clarity and purpose in our discussions.

Imagine a scenario where a couple decides to discuss their differing views on financial management. After dinner, they agree to do so in their living room, a neutral space where both feel comfortable and at ease, to ensure neither is distracted by hunger or the day's fatigue. They start with a mutual acknowledgment of the importance of the conversation and a commitment to abide by their established rules. This simple yet intentional setup lays the groundwork for a productive and respectful dialogue.

Respecting Boundaries

Understanding and honoring each other's emotional and psychological boundaries is crucial during conflicts. These boundaries, unique to each individual, define the limits of what they consider acceptable and safe in interactions. When a partner needs to pause the conversation, this request must be met with respect, recognizing it as a necessary step for emotional regulation rather than an evasion of the issue. This might mean agreeing to continue the conversation the next day when both partners feel more centered and less reactive.

The Importance of Timing

Choosing the right moment to address a disagreement significantly influences the conversation's outcome. Attempting to resolve a conflict when one partner is exhausted from a long day's work or when both are already stressed from an unrelated issue sets the stage for heightened emotions and decreased empathy. In this context, timing becomes a strategic choice, a recognition that the state of our minds and hearts profoundly impacts our ability to engage constructively in difficult conversations.

Staying on Topic

One of the most common pitfalls in conflict resolution is the tendency to veer off-topic, dredging up past grievances or branching into unrelated issues. This diffusion not only dilutes the focus of the conversation but can also escalate the conflict, introducing more points of contention. A strategy to counter this is using a physical or metaphorical "talking stick"—an object granting the holder the sole right to speak, ensuring the conversation remains focused on the issue at hand. This practice, borrowed from indigenous talking circles, emphasizes the importance of listening and respect, anchoring the dialogue in the present and the specific issue being addressed.

In embracing these practices, we recognize that the true measure of a relationship's strength lies not in the absence of conflict but in the ability to engage with it constructively, with empathy, respect, and an unwavering commitment to mutual growth. Through the establishment of rules and boundaries, the careful choice of timing, and the discipline to stay focused on the issue at hand, we forge a path through disagreements that lead not to division but to deeper understanding and harmony.

The Win-Win Approach to Resolving Disputes

In conflict resolution, the concept of win-win solutions emerges as the best of outcomes, offering a path where both partners emerge not merely unscathed but enriched. This paradigm shift from traditional win-lose scenarios, where one partner's gain is perceived as the other's loss, to a framework where both individuals find satisfaction and fulfillment, marks a significant evolution in dispute resolution strategies. At its core, a win-win solution is predicated on the belief that the relationship itself is the entity most deserving of victory and that resolutions can be crafted that honor the needs and desires of both parties involved through collaborative effort. This approach is not about compromise in the traditional sense, where each party gives up something reluctantly, but about finding solutions that genuinely satisfy the core needs of both individuals, thereby enhancing the strength and resilience of their bond.

Developing and applying negotiation skills are pivotal in navigating the journey toward win-win outcomes. Effective negotiation in a relationship transcends the mere exchange of words and demands; it requires an in-depth understanding of one's own needs and an empathetic grasp of the partner's perspectives. Active listening, a skill highlighted for importance in earlier discussions, plays a crucial role here, ensuring that each partner feels heard and validated. Beyond this, the art of negotiation in intimate relationships involves expressing needs and desires in a clear manner, yet imbued with sensitivity to the emotional undercurrents of the dialogue. Techniques such as "I feel" statements, which articulate personal emotions without attributing blame, and the strategic use of pauses, allowing both partners to process information and regulate their emotional responses, are instrumental in fostering an atmosphere conducive to constructive negotiation.

Creative problem-solving invites couples to step outside the confines of conventional thinking, exploring innovative avenues to meet their needs. This process is inherently dynamic, encouraging a departure from rigid positions to the exploration of possibilities that might have previously been obscured by emotional barriers or entrenched patterns of thinking. It involves a willingness to experiment with solutions and entertain ideas that, at first glance, might seem unconventional but, upon deeper reflection, offer the potential to meet the underlying needs of both partners. For example, a couple grappling with allocating household responsibilities might move beyond simple task division to consider solutions like alternating responsibility based on workload or even outsourcing certain tasks to create more quality time together. Such creative approaches not only address the immediate issue but also contribute to a culture of innovation and flexibility within the relationship, qualities that are invaluable in navigating future challenges.

The act of celebrating compromise as a victory for the relationship underscores the inherent value of collaborative conflict resolution. In this context, compromise is not seen as a concession or loss but as a testament to the couple's commitment to the health and longevity of their partnership. This reframe shifts the narrative around conflict, transforming it into an opportunity for mutual growth and deeper understanding. Celebrating these moments, perhaps through a shared activity or simple acknowledgment of the effort and love that went into reaching the resolution, reinforces the positive dynamics of negotiation and compromise. It serves as a reminder that in intimate relationships, victories are measured not by the triumph of one perspective over another but by the ability of both partners to find common ground and grow closer through resolving their disagreements.

Navigating the pathways of conflict within intimate relationships, the win-win approach stands out as a loving and nurturing option, offering strategies that foster respect, understanding, and mutual satisfaction. Through the cultivation of negotiation skills, the embrace of creative problem-solving, and the celebration of compromise, couples can transform the challenges of conflict into stepping stones toward a stronger, more resilient union. This journey, though marked by the inevitable bumps and turns of shared life, is rich with opportunities for growth, connection, and the deepening of love.

Apologies and Forgiveness: Healing After Conflict

The aftermath of a dispute carries the weight of unspoken words and unresolved emotions, lingering like the quiet before a storm. In this charged atmosphere, the act of offering a genuine apology stands out as an honest and sincere gesture, seeking to soothe the pain and confusion. An apology, when rooted in sincerity, acts as a bridge, facilitating the journey from discord back to harmony. Its power lies not in the mere utterance of words but in the acknowledgment of one's actions and their impact on the other. This acknowledgment, coupled with an expression of regret and a commitment to change, forms the cornerstone of a genuine apology. It signals a readiness to mend what has been broken, to step into the vulnerability of admitting fault, and to shoulder the responsibility for healing the breach. This process is far from superficial; it demands introspection, courage, and a deep-seated respect for the bond shared with the partner.

The willingness to accept responsibility for one's part in a conflict transcends the act of apology; it is a testament to the maturity and strength of the relationship. This acceptance is not about assigning blame but about recognizing the interplay of actions and reactions that contribute to a dispute. It requires a shift from defensiveness to openness, from justification to understanding. In doing so, it paves the way for dialogues that aim not to vindicate but to heal, to find a common ground where both partners feel seen and heard. The act of genuinely taking responsibility fosters an environment of trust and safety, essential for the process of forgiveness to begin. It is a step toward dismantling the walls erected by conflict, inviting a return to intimacy and connection.

Forgiveness, in its essence, is the act of releasing resentment, the conscious decision to let go of grievances and to look toward the future with hope rather than backward with bitterness. This process is deeply personal and varies in its timeline and manifestation. It involves a deliberate effort to understand the circumstances that led to the conflict, to empathize with the partner's perspective, and to accept the imperfections inherent in human nature. Forgiveness does not imply forgetting or condoning the hurtful behavior; rather, it signifies a readiness to move forward, to rebuild trust on the foundations of compassion and mutual respect. This journey towards forgiveness is often nonlinear, marked by moments of doubt and resurgence of pain. Yet, with patience and commitment, it leads to a place of greater strength and understanding within the relationship, a testament to the resilience and depth of the bond shared between partners.

The task of rebuilding after a dispute requires a concerted effort, a conscious decision to mend the connection that has been frayed by conflict. This rebuilding is not merely about restoring the status quo but about strengthening the relationship, making it more resilient and more attuned to the needs and sensitivities of both partners. Strategies to facilitate this process encompass a range of actions, from tangible gestures of affection to the reaffirmation of commitment through words and deeds. It involves creating opportunities for shared experiences that reignite joy and intimacy, be it through a hobby that both partners enjoy or simply spending quality time together. Equally important is the commitment to open communication, to continue the dialogue about each other's needs, fears, and aspirations. This ongoing conversation ensures that the lessons learned from the conflict are integrated into the fabric of the relationship, transforming challenges into opportunities for growth and deepening the mutual understanding that forms the bedrock of love and partnership.

Moving through the challenging path of apologies and forgiveness, the journey from conflict to reconciliation unfolds in layers, revealing the human connection's strength, vulnerability, and beauty. It is a path marked by humility, courage, and an unwavering commitment to each other, a reaffirmation of the choice to walk together, hand in hand, through the complexities of life. Through this process, partners learn not only about the resilience of their bond but also about the transformative power of empathy, compassion, and unconditional love.

Creating a Conflict Resolution Plan Together

Creating a customized conflict resolution plan becomes a crucial step in the complex interplay of a relationship, where each interaction contributes to the overall dynamics between partners. This strategic blueprint, tailored to a couple's relationship's unique rhythm and dynamics, serves as a compass through the tempests of discord, guiding both partners back to the sanctuary of understanding and harmony. Crafting such a plan demands a deep dive into the reservoirs of individual and collective experiences and a commitment to nurturing a culture of open dialogue and mutual respect.

The inception of this planning process begins with a candid exploration of past conflicts, identifying patterns, triggers, and resolutions that have either mended or further frayed the threads of connection. This reflective journey, though potentially filled with discomfort, lays the groundwork for a plan that addresses the symptoms of discord and seeks to heal its root causes. In this collaborative endeavor, both partners contribute insights, fears, and aspirations, weaving together a comprehensive strategy that acknowledges their vulnerabilities while capitalizing on their strengths.

The integration of techniques gleaned from the journey thus far into the conflict resolution plan stands as a testament to the couple's growth and learning. Techniques such as active listening, the art of genuine apology, and the pursuit of win-win solutions are not mere tactics but reflections of a deeper commitment to the health and longevity of the relationship. Once abstract concepts, these strategies become concrete actions embedded in the plan, serving as touchstones in times of turmoil. The plan may outline specific steps to de-escalate tensions, mechanisms for initiating and navigating difficult conversations, and rituals to reaffirm connection and affection in the aftermath of a dispute. Each element of the plan not only addresses the logistical aspects of conflict resolution but also honors both partners' emotional and psychological needs.

Recognizing the fluid nature of relationships, the plan includes regular review and adjustment provisions. This ongoing evaluation, perhaps scheduled during moments of calm or as part of a periodic relationship 'check-up,' ensures that the plan remains relevant and responsive to the evolving dynamics of the partnership. It acknowledges that as individuals grow and change, so too do their needs, fears, and ways of relating. Adjustments to the plan may range from introducing new conflict resolution techniques to reevaluating boundaries and rules for engagement. This iterative process underscores the notion that conflict resolution is not a static endeavor but a dynamic aspect of a thriving relationship.

There comes a point in the arc of every relationship when the tools at one's disposal and the strategies within one's plan may not suffice to bridge the chasms of misunderstanding and hurt. In such instances, seeking professional help represents not a defeat but a courageous step towards healing and growth. This acknowledgment that some conflicts may require mediation by an experienced therapist or counselor is woven into the fabric of the plan, offering a pathway to external support when internal resources are stretched thin. Professional guidance provides a neutral perspective on entrenched conflicts and introduces new strategies and insights to enrich the couple's conflict resolution toolkit. This openness to external support mirrors the plan's overarching aim: to fortify the relationship against the inevitable storms of discord, ensuring that each challenge navigated together strengthens the bonds of love and understanding.

In executing this plan, couples embark on a journey that transcends the mere management of disagreements, venturing into the realm of deliberate, conscious partnership. It is a journey marked by moments of vulnerability and strength, of conflict and reconciliation, each step informed by the lessons of the past and the hopes for the future. Through creating, implementing, and regularly revising their personalized conflict resolution plan, partners lay the foundations for a relationship characterized by resilience, empathy, and a deep-seated commitment to navigating life's challenges together.

As we draw this exploration of conflict resolution to a close, we are reminded of the transformative power of intentional, compassionate engagement with the challenges that arise within our most intimate bonds. The strategies and insights shared in this discourse are not mere tools for navigating discord but are, at their core, expressions of the profound love, respect, and commitment that underpin a thriving partnership. In embracing these principles, we enrich our relationships and contribute to a larger tapestry of understanding and connection that transcends the personal to touch the universal.

Now, as we move forward, let us carry with us the knowledge that in the alchemy of human connection, it is through the crucible of conflict that the purest gold of intimacy and understanding is refined.

The Alchemy of Emotional Intimacy

The world is awash with fleeting connections and superficial engagements, but the quest for emotional intimacy is a unique desire for those seeking depth and meaning in their relationships. This profound connection, rooted in understanding, trust, and shared vulnerability, transcends the mere exchange of words, flourishing in the silent spaces between them. In the interaction of hearts and souls laid bare, it is here that the true essence of a partnership is revealed and nurtured.

What is Emotional Intimacy and Why It Matters

Defining Emotional Intimacy

Emotional intimacy is the shared experience of understanding, care, and love that binds two people beyond the surface level of interaction. It's a state where hearts communicate without words, silence speaks volumes, and a glance conveys a thousand emotions. Imagine sitting beside your partner during a moment of shared silence, perhaps watching the sun dip below the horizon. This silence, far from uncomfortable, is a testament to the depth of your connection, a space where each breath and heartbeat is in harmony with the other's. Emotional intimacy is this and more; it's the foundation upon which trust, understanding, and lasting bonds are built.

The Importance of Relationship Health

Emotional intimacy is not just beneficial; it's crucial for the health of any deep, enduring relationship. It is the glue that holds partners together, transforming a collection of moments into a tapestry of shared life. Without it, relationships risk becoming shells of their potential, lacking the warmth and connection that define true companionship. It fosters a sense of belonging, a safe haven where each individual is seen, heard, and valued. This mutual respect and understanding make life's challenges bearable, knowing that you're not facing them alone but hand in hand with someone who truly understands you.

Differentiating from Physical Intimacy

While often intertwined and frequently misdefined, emotional intimacy and physical intimacy are distinct entities, each with its own value and significance. Physical intimacy, with its tactile expressions of love and desire, is undeniably important. Yet, without the foundation of emotional intimacy, these physical expressions risk becoming hollow gestures, devoid of the depth and meaning that fill them with real power. Emotional intimacy enriches physical connections, giving each touch and each kiss layers of shared experiences and understanding. It's the difference between a hug that's merely a hug and one that feels like coming home.

Building a Foundation for Trust

Trust, the cornerstone of any enduring relationship, finds its roots in emotional intimacy. It's born in moments of shared vulnerability, where fears, hopes, and dreams are laid bare, met not with judgment but with acceptance and understanding. This trust is not given lightly; it's earned through consistent, honest communication and the reassurance that comes from knowing your partner truly sees you for who you are. When emotional intimacy is anchored in trust, it becomes a resilient force, capable of weathering the storms of doubt and conflict that invariably arise.

Emotional intimacy, with its intricate blend of understanding, trust, and shared vulnerability, is a testament to deep connections' transformative power. It is both a journey and a destination, a continuous process of discovery and growth that enriches both individuals and their relationship. In the following chapters, we explore the facets of this profound connection, offering insights, strategies, and exercises designed to nurture and deepen the bonds of emotional intimacy.

Exercises to Build Emotional Connection

Cultivating an environment where emotional intimacy flourishes requires deliberate, consistent action. Among the plethora of activities available, certain practices stand out for their efficacy in deepening the emotional bond between partners, transforming the mundane into moments of profound connection.

Daily Check-Ins

The act of engaging in daily check-ins transcends the routine exchange of information about the day's events. It is a sacred ritual, offering one's experiences, feelings, and innermost thoughts to the other. This practice is a conduit for emotional support and understanding when engaged with intentionality. Each partner, in turn, shares the highs and lows of their day, not merely as a recount but as an invitation into their emotional world. The listener, with empathy and undivided attention, receives these offerings, acknowledging them without judgment or unsolicited advice. This reciprocal exchange fosters a climate of trust and safety, where each individual feels seen and heard, reinforcing the emotional foundation of the relationship.

Shared Journaling

Introducing shared journaling into the fabric of a relationship invites a new layer of intimacy, an exploration of thoughts and emotions through the written word. This practice allows for expressing sentiments that might otherwise remain unspoken, hidden beneath layers of hesitation or vulnerability. Partners may choose to write entries independently, reflecting on their feelings, dreams, and desires, then share these writings with one another, or they might engage in a collaborative journaling activity, crafting a narrative of their relationship journey together. The act of reading and reflecting on each other's words opens a window into the soul, offering insights and understanding that deepen the bond between them. Shared journaling serves as a testament to the evolution of the relationship and as a treasure trove of shared memories and emotions, a tangible manifestation of their emotional connection.

Dream Sharing

Creating a space for dream-sharing invites partners into a realm where individual and collective aspirations are nurtured. This practice, far removed from the constraints of everyday realities, fosters a sense of possibility and mutual support. Within this sacred space, dreams are not scrutinized for feasibility or practicality; instead, they are celebrated as expressions of each partner's deepest desires and aspirations. By sharing these visions of the future, partners offer support and encouragement to one another and also engage in a creative exploration of potential paths their shared life could take. Dream sharing becomes a source of inspiration, a reminder of the hopes and possibilities that lie at the heart of the relationship, strengthening the emotional connection through a shared commitment to each other's fulfillment and happiness.

Gratitude Lists

The ritual of sharing daily gratitude lists is an antidote to the negativity bias that often pervades our perception, redirecting focus towards appreciation and acknowledgment. This simple yet profound practice involves each partner listing aspects of their relationship and each other for which they are grateful. These lists shared aloud or through the written exchange, serve as reminders of the beauty and richness of their shared life, highlighting moments of kindness, acts of love, and qualities in each other that evoke gratitude. By regularly acknowledging and expressing gratitude for each other and the relationship, partners reinforce positive emotions and appreciation, countering tendencies toward taking one another for granted. This ritual enhances emotional intimacy by fostering an atmosphere of positivity and appreciation and contributes to a deeper sense of contentment and satisfaction within the relationship.

By integrating these practices into the substance of their relationship, partners deliberately cultivate emotional intimacy. Each exercise, from daily check-ins to sharing gratitude lists, offers a unique avenue for deepening the emotional connection, transforming everyday interactions into opportunities for growth and understanding. Through these practices, partners reinforce the foundation of their relationship, ensuring that the bond of emotional intimacy continues to thrive amidst the ebb and flow of life's challenges.

Overcoming Barriers to Emotional Intimacy

The path toward deep emotional intimacy is often filled with hurdles that, if left unaddressed, can morph into insurmountable walls. These barriers, ranging from the shadows of past traumas to the icy grip of vulnerability, demand not only recognition but a concerted effort to dismantle them.

Identifying Common Barriers

The first step in this endeavor requires a meticulous examination of the barriers obstructing emotional connectivity. Past traumas act as silent sentinels, their presence a constant reminder of the pain that once was, shaping reactions and expectations in ways that often elude conscious understanding. Similarly, the fear of vulnerability, the apprehension of exposing one's true self only to face potential judgment or rejection, can stifle the openness required for intimacy to flourish. Communication issues further complicate the landscape, with misinterpretations and unsaid words adding layers of confusion and distance. Recognizing these barriers is like mapping the terrain of one's emotional landscape, a necessary precursor to navigating through it.

Communication Skills for Vulnerability

Developing and honing communication skills tailored to the delicate task of conveying vulnerabilities are paramount. This involves not just the courage to bare one's soul but the ability to do so in a manner that invites understanding rather than defense. Techniques such as framing disclosures with clarity and directness while avoiding accusations allow for a gentler reception of one's innermost fears and desires. Moreover, the practice of active listening, wherein one listens to respond and understand rather than to rebut or dismiss, serves as a critical counterpart in this dialogue, ensuring that the sharing of vulnerabilities becomes a bridge to closeness rather than a wedge of division.

Healing Past Wounds

Past wounds, with their tenacious grip on the present, necessitate a process of healing that is both profound and, at times, protracted. This journey towards healing requires an environment of unwavering support and patience, where past hurts can be excavated, examined, and ultimately, exorcised. Couples might find themselves embarking on this path through shared therapeutic experiences, guided by professionals who can navigate the complexities of individual and shared traumas. Alternatively, practices such as mutual storytelling, where experiences and the emotions they evoke are shared in a space of safety and acceptance, can facilitate a process of mutual healing. This act of collective vulnerability and support not only aids in mending old wounds but also in fortifying the relationship against future adversities.

Creating a Culture of Acceptance

At the heart of overcoming barriers to emotional intimacy lies the imperative to foster a culture of acceptance within the relationship. This culture is characterized by an unconditional affirmation of each other's emotions, desires, and fears, irrespective of their nature or intensity. It is a realm where all emotions are acknowledged as valid and important, where feelings are encouraged rather than suppressed. Establishing this culture requires consistent effort from both partners, manifested in daily interactions and the broader ethos of the relationship. It involves the deliberate cultivation of an environment where vulnerabilities are not just tolerated but embraced, where sharing one's inner world is met with empathy and love rather than judgment or indifference. This acceptance acts as the fertile soil in which the seeds of emotional intimacy can take root, grow, and blossom into a profound and enduring connection.

The recognition and dismantling of barriers, the artful communication of vulnerabilities, the healing of past wounds, and the creation of a culture of acceptance are not merely steps but intertwined strands that form the fabric of deep emotional connection. Each element, with its nuances and demands, contributes to weaving a relationship tapestry rich with the colors of understanding, trust, and shared vulnerability. Through this intricate process, partners not only navigate the challenges that obstruct their path to intimacy but also lay the groundwork for a bond that is resilient, deep, and imbued with the warmth of genuine connection.

Maintaining Emotional Intimacy Through Life's Challenges

Adapting to life's fluctuations stands as a testament to a couple's resilience, particularly in maintaining the vibrancy of emotional intimacy amidst the ebb and flow of circumstances. The ability to stay connected, to foster warmth and understanding despite the whirlwinds of change, marks a relationship's strength. This adaptability requires an openness to evolve together, to recalibrate expectations, and to navigate through periods of transition, be it career changes, health issues, or the growth of a family. Through these shifts, the continuous sharing of feelings, fears, and hopes acts as a lifeline, keeping partners anchored to each other. It involves the willingness to support each other through these changes and the flexibility to grow individually within the shared space of the relationship. This dynamic balance ensures that emotional intimacy remains a constant, a beacon of connection that endures through the seasons of life.

In the crucible of adversity, emotional intimacy bonds are tested and fortified. Stress, grief, and conflict, while inherently challenging, also offer opportunities for deepening understanding and connection. The key lies in the commitment to turn towards each other, rather than away, during these tough times. Strategies such as maintaining open lines of communication and allowing each partner to express their emotions without fear of judgment or reprisal become crucial. Equally important is the practice of empathy, the effort to truly understand and share in each other's experiences, which can transform adversity into a shared journey of mutual support. This commitment to face life's trials together, to offer comfort and solace in moments of need, strengthens the fabric of the relationship, creating a closeness and trust that are resilient in the face of hardship.

Rituals, those repeated acts filled with meaning and affection, serve as the heartbeat of a relationship, sustaining emotional intimacy through the constancy of shared experiences. Establishing daily or weekly rituals, whether it's a morning coffee together, a nightly walk, or a shared activity that both partners enjoy, creates touchpoints of connection. Simple yet profound rituals become sanctuaries of togetherness, moments where the world outside recedes, allowing partners to reconnect and reaffirm their bond. They act as reminders of the joy and love that underpin the relationship, offering respite and renewal amidst the demands of daily life. As these rituals evolve and adapt over time, they continue to reflect the changing contours of the relationship, anchoring partners in a sense of shared history and mutual commitment.

At times, the internal resources of a couple, no matter how deep or strong, may reach their limits, necessitating the seeking of external support. Counseling or therapy, far from a last resort, represents a proactive step towards nurturing and safeguarding emotional intimacy. These avenues offer a space for exploration and understanding, guided by a neutral professional who can shed light on patterns, dynamics, and strategies that couples may not discern on their own. Whether it's navigating through a significant crisis, addressing long-standing issues, or simply seeking to enhance the quality of the relationship, external support can provide invaluable insights and tools. This openness to guidance reflects a deep commitment to the health and longevity of the relationship, a recognition that sometimes, the path to deeper connection and understanding requires a helping hand.

In genuine and enduring relationships, emotional intimacy is crafted from the moments shared, the obstacles overcome, and the changes navigated side by side. This rich, intimate connection is continuously shaped by the collective journey of a couple, embedding resilience and unity in its very essence. Maintaining this intimacy amidst life's inevitable changes and challenges demands adaptability, commitment, and the willingness to support each other through adversity. The establishment of rituals and the seeking of external support, when necessary, further strengthen this bond, ensuring that emotional intimacy remains a vibrant and enduring facet of the relationship.

As we close this exploration of maintaining emotional intimacy through life's challenges, it becomes clear that the essence of a deeply connected relationship lies not in the absence of adversity but in the shared commitment to navigate through it together. The strategies and insights offered here serve as beacons, guiding couples through the complexities of sustaining closeness and understanding in the face of life's inevitable changes. Looking ahead, the journey continues, with each step offering new opportunities for growth, connection, and the deepening of the bonds that unite us.

Make a Difference with Your Review
Unlock the Power of Generosity

"True happiness comes from giving and helping others."

— Unknown

People who give without expecting anything in return live longer, happier lives. They also find more success in what they do. So, if we have a chance to make a difference together, I'm all for it!

To make that happen, I have a question for you...

Would you help someone you've never met, even if you never got credit for it?

Who is this person, you ask? They are like you, or maybe like you used to be. They want to make their relationship better, but they aren't sure where to start.

Our mission is to make The Complete Relationship Guide for Couples accessible to everyone. Everything I do stems from that mission. And the only way to accomplish that mission is by reaching…well…everyone.

This is where you come in. Most people do, in fact, judge a book by its cover (and its reviews). So here's my ask on behalf of a couple you've never met:

Please help that couple by leaving this book a review.

Your gift costs no money and takes less than 60 seconds, but it can change a couple's life forever. Your review could help…

...one more couple understand each other better.
...one more family find happiness.
...one more person feel loved and valued.
...one more dream come true.

To get that 'feel good' feeling and help this couple for real, all you have to do is...and it takes less than 60 seconds... leave a review.

Simply scan the QR code below to leave your review:

If you feel good about helping a faceless, nameless couple, you are my kind of person. Welcome to the club. You're one of us.

If you feel good about helping a faceless, nameless couple, you are my kind of person. Welcome to the club. You're one of us.

I'm that much more excited to help you grow and deepen your relationship more than you can possibly imagine. You'll love the lessons and insights I'm about to share in the coming chapters.

Thank you from the bottom of my heart. Now, back to our regularly scheduled program.

- Your biggest fan, Riley

PS - Fun fact: If you provide something of value to another person, it makes you more valuable to them. If you believe this book will help another couple, send this book their way.

Fostering Physical Connection and Intimacy

In the complex dance of relationships, physical touch plays a unique role, serving as a quiet yet powerful form of communication that conveys love, desire, and togetherness. This silent dialogue, expressed through the brush of fingers, the warmth of an embrace, or the gentle pressure of a kiss, speaks volumes about the bond between partners. In its myriad forms, physical intimacy brings a closeness that, when nurtured with intention and understanding, can deepen a relationship beyond the surface level of mere attraction or routine.

Understanding Each Other's Physical Needs

Communicating About Physical Needs

Open dialogue about physical needs and desires is the cornerstone of a healthy, intimate relationship. It's akin to setting the stage for a play where both actors know their roles and understand the script, ensuring a performance that resonates with harmony and mutual satisfaction. Discussing physical needs requires a space free from judgment, where honesty flourishes, and vulnerability is met with empathy. It's about sharing what touches warm the heart, which caresses ignite desire, and what boundaries need respect. This conversation might unfold on a quiet evening at home, where distractions are set aside, allowing both partners to listen, understand, and appreciate the unique languages of each other's bodies.

The Spectrum of Physical Intimacy

Physical intimacy spans a broad spectrum, from the tender touch that comforts in times of distress to the passionate embrace that speaks of deep longing. Recognizing this variety is crucial, as it underscores the understanding that intimacy is not just one action or behavior, but diverse and layered. Like the colors of a sunset, each hue contributes to the beauty of the whole, which is essential in creating the masterpiece of a couple's intimate life. Acknowledging this spectrum encourages partners to explore the full range of physical expressions of love, ensuring that intimacy remains vibrant and fulfilling.

Respecting Boundaries

Respect for personal boundaries is the bedrock upon which safe, fulfilling physical intimacy is built. It's the understanding that each person's comfort levels and desires are unique and must be honored. This respect transforms the physical connection into a sanctuary of trust, where each touch and embrace is an affirmation of love and care. Setting and communicating these boundaries can be as straightforward as a conversation before a moment of intimacy, laying the groundwork for a relationship where both partners feel valued and understood.

Physical Affection to Express Love

For many, physical touch is a primary and significant means through which love is most profoundly expressed and understood. It's the hand held under the table during dinner, the hug that melts away a day's stress, or the gentle kiss that says, "I'm here for you." These gestures, small in execution but vast in significance, are constant reminders of love and connection. Recognizing and embracing physical touch as a primary means to express love enriches the relationship, allowing both partners to feel loved in the way that resonates most deeply with them.

With all physical intimacy, the emphasis on open communication, understanding the spectrum of intimacy, respecting boundaries, and recognizing physical touch as a love language paves the way for a relationship where physical connection deepens emotional bonds. This approach ensures that physical intimacy remains a source of joy, comfort, and expression of love, enriching the relationship in profound and lasting ways.

The Role of Affection in a Healthy Relationship

Within a thriving partnership, non-sexual physical affection emerges as a pivotal facet, its significance often overshadowed by the more overt expressions of love. Yet, in relationships, actions such as cuddling, kissing, and the simple act of touching hold an understated power, knitting partners closer in silent communication that transcends words. This subtle yet profound connection is a constant reminder of the warmth and care that pulses at the heart of the partnership, a tangible manifestation of love that nourishes both individuals.

The essence of affection extends beyond the realms of sexual intimacy, inhabiting the everyday moments that, while seemingly mundane, are steeped with the potential for deep emotional connection. Consider the gentle brush of fingers as two individuals pass in the hallway of their home, or the comforting embrace that envelops one in a moment of sorrow. These actions, small in execution, are monumental in their impact, binding the emotional with the physical, and reinforcing the foundation upon which a healthy relationship stands. In the absence of these touches, a partnership risks descending into a state of emotional sterility, where the physical distance becomes a chasm too vast to bridge.

In its myriad forms, regular, affectionate touch is a catalyst for feelings of safety, security, and belonging. It signals to each partner that they are not alone and exist within a haven of mutual care and understanding. This sense of security, intangible yet palpable, allows individuals to navigate the vicissitudes of life with the knowledge that they have a steadfast source of support by their side. In moments of vulnerability, the simple act of holding one another can serve as an anchor, grounding both in the present and dispelling the shadows of isolation that often accompany life's trials.

However, the expression and reception of affection are not universal but deeply personal, influenced by cultural backgrounds and individual preferences. Cultural norms, with their unspoken rules and expectations, shape how affection is displayed and interpreted, adding layers of complexity to the ways in which love is communicated. Within this reality, the challenge lies in honoring these differences and in finding a harmonious balance that respects the intricacies of each partner's upbringing and personal comfort levels. This endeavor, a negotiation of sorts, demands sensitivity and an openness to adapt, ensuring that affection remains a source of joy rather than discomfort.

Affection without expectation represents a pure form of love that seeks neither reward nor reciprocation but offers itself freely as an expression of care. In a culture where physical touch is often entangled with sexual desire, distinguishing between the two becomes essential, allowing for a space where affection is given and received as a standalone gift of love. This distinction fosters a culture of care within the relationship, where each gesture of affection is imbued with the simple intent to convey love and appreciation. It liberates physical touch from the confines of expectation, transforming it into a pure connection that profoundly enriches the relationship.

In the realm of love and partnership, the role of non-sexual physical affection stands as a testament to the power of touch, a language that communicates the depth of feeling that words often fail to capture. It is a reminder that within the complexities of a relationship, the simplest acts of affection hold the potential to deepen the bond to weave a resilient, warm, and enduring fabric of connection. Through the conscious cultivation of this form of intimacy, partners enhance their relationship and affirm the beauty of their shared journey, a journey marked by the silent songs of touch that resonate with love and care.

Navigating Differences in Desire

Where hearts intertwine and passions burn with varied intensities, the discrepancies in sexual desire between partners emerge as silent rivers that, if left unbridged, can carve canyons within the landscape of intimacy. This divergence, natural as it may be, holds the potential to create hurt, transforming serene days into turbulent storms, should understanding and empathy fail to be engaged. The recognition of these differences not as flaws but as facets of the multifaceted gem of a relationship is the initial step towards harmonizing the discord of individual desires into a symphony of mutual satisfaction.

Addressing this variance demands an open-hearted conversation where shame and blame have no place. Such dialogues are delicate endeavors, requiring a language that eschews accusation for understanding, that replaces judgment with curiosity. Partners must approach these discussions with the knowledge that desire is influenced by a myriad of factors, from the physiological to the psychological, from the stressors of daily life to the shadows of past experiences. Engaging in these conversations with honesty and vulnerability paves the way for a deeper connection, where differences in desire are met without frustration but with compassion and a shared commitment to navigate the complexities together.

The quest for a middle ground, where the needs and desires of both partners are honored, is an exercise in creativity and compromise. This endeavor is less about concession and more about exploration, about uncovering new forms of intimacy that satisfy both the craving for closeness and the need for individual expression. Suggestions for navigating this terrain might include scheduling intimate encounters, thereby removing the pressure of spontaneity for the partner with lower desire, while providing a space of anticipation for the one with higher desire. Similarly, expanding the definition of intimacy to include a broader spectrum of physical and emotional connections can satisfy the need for closeness without placing undue emphasis on sexual activity. Through these creative adjustments, partners can cultivate intimacy that flourishes with of mutual satisfaction.

Central to the harmonization of differing desires is the cultivation of emotional intimacy. This deep, invisible link found throughout the heart of the relationship acts as a catalyst, transforming the physical expression of love into an experience that transcends the mere act, enriching it with layers of meaning and connection. Emotional intimacy, nurtured through shared experiences, open communication, and the continual affirmation of love and appreciation, is fertile soil where physical desire can be realized. It is in the moments of laughter shared over a meal, in the tears shed in each other's arms, in the quiet support offered without question, that desire finds new breath, invigorated not by the physical alone but by the profound bond of shared life. Thus, the deepening of emotional intimacy becomes a path to understanding and reconciling differences in physical desire and a journey towards a more fulfilling union, where the physical and emotional intertwine in a dance of enduring passion and love.

Within the intricacies of desire, where differences emerge as both challenge and opportunity, the journey towards understanding, empathy, and compromise unfolds as a testament to the strength and depth of the relationship. It is a journey that demands courage, creativity, and a commitment to each other's happiness, where the goal is not merely the realization of love and intimacy. The variation in sexual desire between partners often emerges as a subtle undercurrent that, if not mindfully bridged, can gradually erode the foundation of closeness. Such differences, though entirely natural, have the potential to create emotional distance if not approached with compassion and open-mindedness. Recognizing these variations not as shortcomings but as inherent aspects of a complex relationship marks the first step towards blending these distinct rhythms into a harmonious melody of mutual fulfillment. Embarking on this journey requires engaging in candid conversations where guilt and blame are conspicuously absent. These discussions are nuanced, demanding a language that prioritizes empathy over accusation and curiosity over judgment. It's essential for partners to acknowledge that desire is a dynamic and elusive force, shaped by a wide array of influences ranging from biological factors to psychological intricacies, and from daily stressors to the echoes of past traumas. Approaching these dialogues with honesty and openness lays the groundwork for a stronger bond, where disparities in desire are met with understanding and a collective resolve to confront these challenges together. Finding a balance that respects the wishes and needs of both individuals is an exercise in creativity and compromise. This process is less about making sacrifices and more about discovery, about venturing into new realms of intimacy that fulfill both the yearning for connection and the longing for personal space. Strategies for navigating this path may involve scheduling moments of intimacy, which alleviates the pressure of spontaneity for the partner with lesser desire and builds a sense of anticipation for the one with greater desire. Broadening the definition of intimacy to encompass various forms of physical and emotional connection can also help meet the need for closeness without overemphasizing sexual encounters. Through such innovative adjustments, partners can nurture a relationship that thrives on mutual contentment. At the heart of aligning divergent desires is the deepening of emotional intimacy. This profound, intangible link that binds the relationship together acts as a catalyst, elevating the physical aspect of love into something that transcends mere action, imbuing it with significance and depth. Emotional intimacy, fostered through shared experiences, transparent communication, and consistent expressions of love and appreciation, provides the fertile ground for desire to grow. In the shared moments of joy, the comforting embraces during sorrow, and the unwavering support offered in silence, desire is rekindled, fueled not only by physical attraction but by the deep, meaningful connection of shared life experiences. Thus, nurturing emotional intimacy is vital for bridging differences in physical desire and embarking on a more profound journey toward a fulfilling partnership, where physical and emotional elements are interwoven in a lasting bond of passion and love. In navigating the complexities of desire, where differences present both challenges and opportunities, the path toward empathy, understanding, and compromise is a testament to the resilience and depth of the relationship. It is a path that requires courage, innovation, and dedication to mutual happiness, aiming not just to reconcile these differences but to foster a deeper, more enriching connection. Through open communication, creative exploration, and the strengthening of emotional bonds, partners can traverse the landscape of differing desires, uncovering new pathways to intimacy and satisfaction that enrich their relationship in immeasurable ways and yield the cultivation of a richer, more satisfying union. Through open dialogue, creative exploration, and the deepening of emotional intimacy, partners can navigate the waters of differing desires, discovering along the way new avenues of connection and satisfaction that enrich their relationship beyond measure.

Creative Ways to Enhance Physical Intimacy

Physical intimacy, with facets of touch, desire, and connection, flourishes in the space of creativity. Within this creative domain, couples find avenues to deepen their bond, transcending the ordinary to discover a realm where every gesture, touch, and caress becomes a testament to their mutual devotion and exploration. This quest for innovation in the realm of physical connection not only reinvigorates the senses but also strengthens the foundational bonds of trust and mutual understanding, ensuring that the physical aspect of the relationship remains vibrant and fulfilling.

Exploring New Experiences Together

The decision to join new physical activities together, such as engaging in dance classes or practicing couples yoga, is a powerful source for enhancing physical closeness. These shared experiences offer more than just the benefits of the activities themselves; they create a shared space of vulnerability and synchronicity, where each movement and breath becomes a step closer to one another. Imagine the gentle guidance of a partner in a yoga pose or the synchronized rhythm of bodies moving in dance—these moments are not merely physical activities but profound connections that echo the harmony and attunement of the relationship. They serve as a reminder that physical intimacy is not confined to the realms of the bedroom but is a vibrant and dynamic aspect of the partnership that extends into all facets of shared life.

Sensual Date Nights

The intentional planning of date nights dedicated to exploring and enhancing sensual experiences opens doors to new dimensions of intimacy. These carefully curated encounters, whether they involve a massage exchange by candlelight or the exploration of new cuisines that tantalize the taste buds, invite couples to immerse themselves in the realm of the senses. Each experience, rich with potential for discovery and pleasure, becomes a journey into the depths of connection, where every touch, taste, and scent is imbued with the essence of the partners' bond. These date nights stand as oases in the desert of routine, spaces where the mundane gives way to the magic of sensory exploration, fostering a deeper appreciation and desire for one another.

Surprise and Spontaneity

Within the landscape of a long-term relationship, the element of surprise acts as a refreshing spring, breathing life into the routine of daily existence. The incorporation of spontaneity into physical expressions of love—be it an unexpected embrace, a surprise kiss, or an impromptu romantic gesture—injects a sense of excitement and anticipation into the relationship. These spontaneous acts of affection, devoid of expectation and rooted in the desire to delight one's partner, are vivid reminders of the depth of feeling and attraction underpinning the relationship. They disrupt the predictability that can sometimes dampen desire, rekindling the flames of passion with the spark of the unexpected, reminding both partners of the joy and thrill of their connection.

Educational Resources

The pursuit of knowledge in the realm of physical intimacy through books, workshops, and courses represents an investment in the growth and development of the relationship. This educational journey, taken together, not only equips couples with new insights and techniques to enhance their physical connection but also deepens their understanding of each other's desires, limitations, and possibilities. It's an exploration that transcends the acquisition of skills, venturing into the realm of mutual discovery, where learning becomes an act of love. Whether it's a workshop on massage techniques, a course on sensual communication, or a book on the art of intimacy, these resources serve as guides on the path to a more fulfilling physical connection, offering new languages of love for couples to explore and master together.

Couples find creativity, exploration, and education as guides in pursuing a richer, more vibrant physical connection. These endeavors, from the shared exploration of new physical activities to the intentional cultivation of surprise and spontaneity, from sensual date nights to the pursuit of knowledge, weave together a tapestry of ever-evolving, ever-deepening intimacy. They remind us that physical intimacy is far from a static aspect of a relationship and a dynamic and creative force, a space of endless possibility and discovery. Through these creative avenues, couples enhance their physical connection and strengthen the bonds of trust, understanding, and mutual respect that form the foundation of their relationship.

As we close this chapter, we reflect on the journey through the realms of physical intimacy, recognizing its role not as a mere component of a relationship but as a vibrant expression of love, connection, and mutual exploration. The paths we've traversed, from understanding each other's physical needs to the creative enhancement of our physical connection, serve as a testament to the depth and richness of the bond shared between partners. They remind us that at the heart of physical intimacy lies the opportunity for growth, discovery, and the continual reaffirmation of our devotion to one another. As we turn our gaze forward, we carry with us the insights and strategies that have illuminated our path, ready to embrace the next chapter in our shared journey with open hearts and minds, ever committed to nurturing the love that binds us together.

Integrating Financial Unity into the Fabric of Love

Within love and partnership, financial matters frequently introduce a challenging note, disrupting the harmonious flow of romance and connection. However, when partners align their financial perspectives, converting discord into harmony, they create a unified vision that enhances their lives together. Money, far from being a mere medium of exchange, becomes a canvas upon which dreams are drawn and futures envisioned. Within this financial journey—lessons embraced, mistakes pardoned, and harmonies aligned—love discovers a steady beat that ensures both endurance and prosperity.

Navigating the idea of joint versus separate finances unveils a facet of life rife with choices, each path forked with its merits and challenges. The decision to merge financial lives, blending incomes, expenses, and dreams into a unified pot, speaks to a deep level of trust and mutual ambition. It's like planting a garden together; both partners must tend to it, mindful of the delicate balance between individual desires and collective needs. Conversely, maintaining separate accounts allows for autonomy and personal space within the broader territory of partnership. This approach mirrors a duo of soloists who, while performing their unique pieces, contribute to the concert's overall beauty. The key lies in striking a chord that resonates with both, ensuring that neither autonomy nor unity stifles the other.

Setting financial goals together, whether pinning down aspirations for a home, travel, or retirement, fosters a sense of unity and purpose. This collaborative venture requires open dialogue, where each voice is heard, and every dream given wings. The act of setting goals becomes a ritual, a reaffirmation of shared commitment and mutual support, where the future is not a distant shore but a horizon eagerly approached side by side.

Transparency in financial matters is the foundation for trust, a cornerstone without which the partnership risks crumbling. Open books symbolize open hearts, where secrets find no shadow to linger. This transparency ensures that decisions are made with a full view of the terrain, informed and intentional. It's not merely about revealing numbers but sharing vulnerabilities, hopes, and fears. Such openness transforms financial planning from a task to a testament of trust, a shared language that strengthens the bond between partners.

Moving through the world of finances, with its jargon and intricacies, can feel like charting unknown waters. Here, financial advisors and planning tools serve as lighthouses, guiding couples safely to their desired destinations. These resources, whether human expertise or digital platforms, offer clarity, transforming complex concepts into actionable steps. They're not just aids but allies in the quest for financial harmony, providing insights that empower couples to make informed decisions that align with their collective vision.

Financial harmony plays a crucial role in the realm of love and partnership, where dreams and practicalities intertwine. It's a dance of numbers and nuances, of dreams deferred and desires fulfilled, a delicate balance between individual autonomy and collective ambition. Through open dialogue, shared goals, transparency, and the wise use of resources, couples can create a financial life that supports and sustains their journey together. It's within this life that love finds a sustaining process that promises growth, security, and a future forged together.

Handling Debt and Financial Disagreements

When dreams and practicality clash and coalesce in the realm of relationships, the specter of debt looms as a formidable challenge, casting long shadows on the paths of partnership. This financial burden, often carried on the shoulders of both, demands a strategy not just of management but of unity, a plan that acknowledges the weight of the load while charting a course toward liberation. Prioritizing high-interest debt emerges as a tactical maneuver in this battle, a decision that minimizes the accrual of interest and maximizes the efficacy of each payment made. Crafting a payoff plan is like laying down the bricks of a road out of the quagmire, a route planned with meticulous care and mutual agreement, ensuring that every step taken is one closer to financial freedom. Similarly, starting with the smallest debt amount, paying it off, and then rolling that minimum payment into the next smallest debt and repeating that process over and over creates the feeling of accomplishment and traction as the number of debt accounts gets fewer and fewer.

Financial disagreements often find places that can tear the heart of the relationship. Navigating these disputes requires a finesse that blends the rational with the emotional, a method that transforms confrontation into conversation. Techniques for this delicate interaction include the establishment of a neutral ground for discussions, a space devoid of the day's tensions, where calm presides, and voices can be heard in their softest tones. Here, active listening becomes a tool of unparalleled worth, allowing each partner to absorb the words and the emotions and fears underpinning them. This approach, coupled with a commitment to seeking solutions rather than assigning blame, paves a path through the thicket of discord, a route marked by understanding and the shared resolve to emerge stronger on the other side.

Compromise and sacrifice, twin pillars in the architecture of partnership, find their true expression in the journey toward mutual financial goals. These concepts, often viewed through the lens of loss, are, in truth, the bedrock of gain, the ground from which the future's dreams sprout. Compromise, in this context, is not about relinquishing dreams but shaping them with reality, fashioning aspirations that can stand firm on practicality. Sacrifice, too, sheds its cloak of negativity, revealing itself as an act of love, a decision to forego the immediate for the promise of the shared tomorrow. In these moments, when one chooses us over the I, the strength of the partnership is forged, tempered in the fires of financial challenges, and cooled in the waters of mutual support.

Establishing emergency funds and financial safety nets acts as a protection against uncertainty, a haven where the relationship can find shelter in times of need. These reserves, built with patience and foresight, serve as reminders of the couple's resilience, tangible evidence of their ability to anticipate and prepare for the unforeseen. The importance of these funds transcends the mere accumulation of capital; it's a practice that reinforces the partnership's commitment to security and stability. In contributing to this shared reserve, both partners engage in an act of faith, a belief in the strength of their bond and their capacity to weather life's vicissitudes together. This preparation, far from an admission of fear, is an affirmation of hope, a declaration that together, they are more than the sum of their individual parts, capable of facing and overcoming life's challenges.

In the complex interaction of love and finances, where dreams meet reality and practical decisions are necessary, developing the skill to tackle debt and financial disagreements is essential. This ability highlights the couple's resilience and flexibility. Through strategies that prioritize unity and understanding, techniques that elevate conversation above confrontation, and commitments to compromise sacrifice, and preparation, couples can navigate the complexities of financial management. This journey, marked by the mutual resolve to build a future free from the burdens of debt, is a reflection of the partnership's depth, a dance of numbers and emotions where love, in its most practical form, finds expression in the shared pursuit of financial harmony.

Budgeting Together for Future Goals

Crafting a joint budget is the cornerstone in building a shared financial future, a careful balance of aspirations and reality, where each expense and saving is a step in their life's journey. More than just distributing funds, this endeavor is a place for dreams, shaped by the practicalities of their financial situation. The initial step requires an unvarnished look at the financial situation, gathering data from bank statements, bills, and receipts that, when pieced together, reveal the actuality of current spending. With this groundwork laid, the task then shifts to a frank discussion about individual necessities, shared responsibilities, and the dreams on the horizon of their collective future. Here, in this confluence of needs and wants, the budget begins to take form, not as a rigid cage but as a flexible framework within which their financial life can flow.

Allocating money to each partner for discretionary spending is an important part of the financial plan. The intent for these dollars, this "fun money" allows for for personal expression within the collective vision, ensuring that individual desires are not lost in the sea of mutual goals. The key lies in mutual respect and communication, in understanding that the vibrancy of their shared picture depends as much on the individual strokes as on the cohesive vision. To this end, setting aside funds for personal pleasures becomes not an act of selfishness but a recognition of the individuality that enriches their partnership. While potentially fraught with tension, these discussions are opportunities for growth, moments where the understanding of each other's values and priorities deepens, reinforcing the fabric of their relationship.

As time unfurls, bringing with it changes in income, expenses, and aspirations; the budget must evolve, an organic document that adapts to the shifting aspects of their financial situation. Regular reviews of this financial blueprint, perhaps quarterly or bi-annually, become milestones in their journey, moments to pause and reflect on their path and the roads that lie ahead. These adjustments, whether in response to a salary increase, an unexpected expense, or a newly minted dream, are crafted with care, ensuring that the budget remains a faithful reflection of their current reality and future aspirations. Through this iterative process, the budget retains its relevance, a faithful guide on their journey toward financial freedom and the fulfillment of their shared dreams.

It's essential to recognize that the budget serves the couple's needs and aspirations, rather than imposing constraints upon them.

In the march towards financial milestones—be it the extinguishing of debt, the acquisition of a home, or the realization of a dream long-held—celebration becomes a vital ritual, a moment to pause and revel in the fruits of their shared labor. These celebrations, whether a simple toast over a homemade dinner or a weekend getaway, are filled with significance, marking not just the achievement of a goal but the strength of their partnership and the efficacy of their teamwork. Such moments serve as reminders of their capacity to conquer challenges and turn aspirations into reality through the alchemy of mutual effort and dedication. These rituals of celebration weave joy and gratitude into the fabric of their financial life, reinforcing the bonds of partnership and imbuing the journey toward future goals with a sense of possibility and anticipation.

In this intricate interplay of numbers and dreams, the act of budgeting together for future goals becomes more than a financial endeavor; it is a declaration of unity and a testament to the strength of their partnership. Through the meticulous planning of a joint budget, the fair allocation of discretionary spending, the adaptive nature of regular budget reviews, and the joyous celebration of financial milestones, couples craft a financial narrative that is uniquely theirs. This narrative, rich with the promise of shared dreams and the triumphs of mutual achievements, becomes a cornerstone of their life together, a testament to the power of love, communication, and teamwork in creating a future filled with hope, security, and fulfillment.

Financial Stress and Its Impact on Relationships

In the interplay of love and finance, stress acts as an uninvited ghost, its presence a silent strain on the bonds that tether hearts together. This specter, often invisible yet palpably felt, weaves its way into the fabric of a relationship, pulling at threads of communication and intimacy until the weave loosens, threatening the unity painstakingly built by two people. Recognizing the harbingers of this stress involves a keen eye for subtle shifts in behavior and dialogue and watchfulness for signs such as a partner's sudden reticence to discuss future plans or an undercurrent of tension when bills or expenses are mentioned. Though seemingly inconsequential in isolation, these indicators collectively paint a picture of a relationship under the weight of financial concern.

To move with love and respect through the fog of this strain requires a strategy that addresses not only the surface symptoms but the emotional underbelly of financial stress. Techniques to alleviate this pressure might include adopting mindfulness practices, where moments of quiet reflection become sanctuaries from the storm of worry. Here, through deep breaths and centered thoughts, partners find a calm within themselves and a steadiness to face financial challenges with clarity. Additionally, fostering an environment where open dialogue about fears and anxieties is encouraged and safe from judgment becomes crucial. In these discussions, vulnerability is not a weakness but a bridge to understanding, a pathway through which support and reassurance flow freely, knitting partners closer in their shared struggle against the tides of uncertainty.

Preemptively shielding the relationship from the ravages of financial stress calls for a proactive stance on managing resources and a commitment to living within one's means while eschewing the siren call of unnecessary debt. This approach, pragmatic yet imbued with a vision for a future unshackled by financial burdens, involves meticulous planning and discipline. Couples might find solace in crafting a budget that mirrors their current realities and future aspirations, a financial blueprint that guides the landscape of income and expenditure. In this act of planning, the focus remains not on deprivation but on mindful allocation, ensuring that each dollar spent contributes to the collective well-being and the fruition of shared dreams.

Yet, there are moments when the mountain of stress seems insurmountable, its shadow casting a pall over the relationship, chilling the warmth that once defined the partnership. In these times, the wisdom to seek external support becomes a reach for hope. Financial advisors, with their expertise and insight, offer guidance through the labyrinth of economic challenges. Similarly, relationship counseling provides a haven for couples to explore the emotional depths of financial stress, a space where feelings of inadequacy, fear, and frustration can be aired and addressed. This dual approach, addressing both the practicalities of finance and the emotional toll it exacts, ensures a comprehensive strategy to weather financial storms. It is a testament to the strength of the partnership, an acknowledgment that seeking help is not an admission of defeat but a declaration of unity in the face of adversity.

As the chapter on financial stress and its impact on relationships draws to a close, we reflect on how important vigilance, open communication, and proactive management are as barriers against the erosive effects of economic strain. Through mindfulness, dialogue, prudent financial planning, and the humility to seek external guidance, couples can fortify their bonds, transforming financial challenges into opportunities for growth and deeper connection. This journey through the realm of finance, fraught with potential pitfalls yet ripe with possibilities, underscores the resilience of love in the face of adversity, a reminder that together, partners can navigate any storm, emerging not just unscathed but stronger, their commitment to each other reaffirmed.

As we transition from the intricacies of finance to the broader landscape of partnership dynamics, the lessons learned from navigating financial stress illuminate the path ahead. The principles of communication, empathy, and joint action form the bedrock upon which a robust, enduring relationship is built, a foundation strong enough to support a partnership through any challenge.

Cultivating and Safeguarding Connection Amidst Life's Transformations

In our world change is the only constant. Navigating the ebbs and flows of career aspirations within the partnership offers both a challenge and an opportunity for growth. Navigating the intersection of professional ambitions and relationship harmony is like balancing on a tightrope, where maintaining equilibrium and fostering open communication are crucial. In this balancing act, couples discover the resilience to back each other's aspirations while protecting the union that binds them together.

Communicating Through Career Changes

Discussing Career Aspirations and Changes

Open dialogue about career aspirations and impending changes lays the foundation for mutual understanding and support. Picture a scenario where one partner dreams of venturing into a new field, a leap filled with uncertainties yet brimming with potential. Such a conversation might unfold on a quiet evening, where the day's distractions fade into the background, allowing dreams and hopes to take center stage. Here, expressions of support and understanding intertwine with practical considerations, creating shared aspirations. The key lies in truly listening to each other's hopes, concerns, and envisioned paths, fostering an environment where dreams are nurtured, not stifled.

Impact of Career Changes on the Relationship

Career changes, with their inherent uncertainties, can create challenges in a relationship, bringing financial strain, time constraints, and stress. Recognizing the multifaceted impact of these shifts is crucial. For example, when one partner decides to pursue further education, the resultant financial strain and reduced time together might test the relationship's resilience. Mitigating these effects requires a proactive approach, identifying potential stressors early and developing strategies collaboratively. This might involve setting aside dedicated time for connection, regardless of the demanding nature of career pursuits, ensuring that the relationship remains a priority amidst the whirlwind of professional growth.

Supporting Each Other's Career Goals

Active support for each other's career goals can take many forms, from the practical to the emotional. It's about more than just words of encouragement; it's about actions demonstrating commitment to each other's success. This could manifest in taking on extra household responsibilities to afford the other partner more time to study or creating a quiet space at home conducive to work. It's also about celebrating milestones, no matter how small, recognizing that each step forward is a victory worth acknowledging. This support becomes a lifeline, a constant amidst the chaos of change, reinforcing the notion that success is sweeter when shared.

Balancing Career and Relationship

Maintaining a healthy balance between career ambitions and nurturing a relationship is an art form. It requires a conscious effort to ensure that the pursuit of professional goals does not overshadow the cultivation of the relationship. Setting boundaries around work time and space can help, as can scheduling regular check-ins and date nights to foster connection. It's similar to tending a garden, where both flowers—the relationship—and vegetables—the career—need water and sunlight to thrive. Neither can be neglected without consequences. Thus, couples must navigate this balance with care, ensuring that as they grow individually, they continue to grow together as well.

While navigating the uncertainty of career changes within the context of a relationship, open communication, mutual support, and a commitment to balance are key. By engaging in honest discussions about aspirations and fears, recognizing the impact of career shifts on the relationship, actively supporting each other's goals, and striving for balance, couples can not only weather the storms of change but emerge stronger, with a deeper connection and a shared sense of purpose. The journey through career changes becomes not just a test of the relationship's resilience but an opportunity for growth, a chance to forge a deeper bond in the crucible of shared challenges and aspirations.

Relocation: Making the Decision Together

Considering a Move

The possibility of relocating for a job opportunity unfurls many considerations, each with implications for the individual, the partner, and the relationship itself. At the heart of this deliberation lies the dual challenge of assessing the professional gains against the personal adjustments required, a balancing act that demands both introspection and empathy. The allure of career advancement or the promise of financial reward must be weighed against the emotional cost of uprooting, the strain of adapting to unfamiliar surroundings, and the impact on the partner's own career trajectory and social well-being. Here, the decision-making calculus extends beyond the tangible metrics of salary increments or career progression to encompass the nuanced dynamics of partnership and mutual fulfillment. It requires an holistic approach, acknowledging that the impact of relocation extends far into the couple's shared life, touching upon aspects as diverse as the partner's professional ambitions, the cohesion of the family unit, and social connections that bind one to a place.

The Relocation Discussion

Engaging in a constructive conversation about relocation transcends the mere logistics of the move, evolving into a dialogue that bridges dreams with reality and aspirations with practicalities. This conversation is anchored in transparency and mutual respect, acknowledging that the decision to relocate is not solitary but a mutual venture, with stakes and consequences for both partners. It is a dialogue that unfolds in the quiet spaces of togetherness, away from the clamor of daily routines, in moments carved out for reflection and connection. Here, the pros and cons are laid bare, not in a spirit of contention but as possibilities, each piece examined for its fit within the couple's aspirations and values. Acknowledging and validating each other's perspectives becomes the cornerstone of this discussion, ensuring that the decision, regardless of its direction, is a product of consensus, a testament to the strength and resilience of the relationship in facing life's crossroads.

Adjusting to a New Place

A new place, with its unfamiliar patterns and routines, creates a new beginning where a couple can start their new journey together. Adjusting to this new environment is a process that unfolds in the shared experiences of exploration and discovery. It involves walking the streets hand in hand, learning the rhythm of the new locale, its sights, sounds, and flavors, each a step of their new life. Building a support network in this novel setting is a crucial task, a deliberate effort to bring new connections into the couple's joint existence. This may involve reaching out to local communities, joining clubs or groups aligned with their interests, or simply forging friendships with neighbors. These connections serve as anchors, providing a sense of belonging and community that can mitigate the initial disorientation and isolation that relocation often brings.

Maintaining Connections

In the wake of relocation, maintaining ties with family and friends left behind is critical to one's identity, ensuring that long-standing relationships continue to flow despite the physical distance. This task requires creativity and commitment, leveraging technology to bridge miles with video calls, messages, and virtual gatherings. It's about marking calendars for visits, whether returning to familiar haunts or inviting loved ones to explore the new home, transforming geographical distance into opportunities for deeper reconnections. These efforts to sustain and nurture existing relationships are not merely acts of reminiscence but affirmations of the enduring nature of bonds that withstand the test of distance and time. They underscore the notion that while landscapes may change, the essence of meaningful connections remains constant, a comforting continuity amidst the flux of new beginnings.

When considering relocation, where the allure of new horizons meets the gravity of established ties, couples navigate a path that is at once daunting and exhilarating. This journey, marked by deliberation, dialogue, and the shared endeavor of adaptation, is not merely about changing geographies but about the evolution of the relationship itself, a testament to its adaptability and enduring strength in the face of life's inevitable shifts.

Supporting Each Other Through Loss and Grief

Understanding Different Grieving Processes

When couples face grief, either together or individually, love and understanding become crucial supports in a dark time. With its myriad expressions and timelines, the individuality of sorrow needs a profound and tender patience. It is not uncommon for partners to find themselves on divergent paths within the labyrinth of loss, where one may seek solace in solitude while the other searches for comfort in shared memories. Recognizing this difference is not an act of division but a profound acknowledgment of each soul's singular journey in the face of loss. This acknowledgment paves the way for a support system that is fluid and adaptable, one that honors the need for space as much as it does the need for closeness. Working through these individual processes with empathy and openness builds the foundation for mutual support, ensuring that the chasm of grief becomes a bridge to deeper understanding.

Communication During Grief

In the midst of grief, words often find themselves inadequate, stumbling in their attempts to convey the depth of sorrow or the longing for what once was. Yet, through communication—imperfect and halting though it may be—connections are reaffirmed in the shadow of loss. The language of grief is one of gestures as much as it is of words; a hand held in silent support, a presence that demands nothing but offers everything. Tips for navigating this delicate dialogue include offering open-ended invitations to share feelings and ensuring that the grieving partner dictates the pace and depth of the conversation. It is also crucial to recognize the value of non-verbal communication, of being present without the pressure of speech, allowing the silence between words to carry the weight of empathy and understanding. This approach fosters an environment where grief is not rushed or dismissed but acknowledged as a profound experience that shapes the contours of the relationship.

Strengthening the Relationship Through Grief

Within the desolation that loss often brings, the resilience and deeper connection can find a place to grow. The shared experience of grief, with its raw vulnerability and unvarnished truth, can act as a crucible in which a relationship's strength is tested and forged. In these moments of shared sorrow, the superficial layers are stripped away, revealing the bedrock of trust and mutual support upon which true partnership is built. Strategies for this journey include the creation of rituals that honor the memory of the lost, providing a shared space for remembrance and healing. It is also important to recognize and celebrate the ways in which the relationship evolves in response to grief, acknowledging the growth that comes from experiencing adversity together. This process, while inherently painful, offers an opportunity to deepen the bond to emerge with a heightened appreciation for the fragility of life and the enduring strength of love.

Seeking External Support

There are moments when the weight of grief exceeds the capacity of a partnership to bear it alone, moments when the shadows grow too deep and the path too obscured. In these times, the decision to seek external support becomes an act of courage, a recognition that the journey through loss is one that need not be undertaken alone. Grief counselors and support groups offer a space where sorrow can be shared and understood by those who have experienced similar losses and those trained in the delicate reality of grieving. This external perspective can provide both a mirror and a map, reflecting the universality of loss while offering guidance on the path through it. It is a choice that underscores the strength of the relationship, an acknowledgment that seeking help is not a relinquishment of responsibility but an expansion of the support network, a testament to the commitment to heal not just as individuals but as partners in life's unpredictable journey.

In this dense exploration of grief within the partnership, the themes of understanding, communication, mutual growth, and seeking external support emerge as a path through loss. They offer a way that, while inevitably marked by sorrow, is also illuminated by the potential for deeper connection, resilience, and a renewed appreciation for the intricate dance of life and love.

Embracing New Roles: Parenthood and Beyond

The transition to parenthood stands as a profound alteration in a couple's life, a change that transforms not only individual identities but also the very substance of the relationship. This pivotal shift usher in a season of new responsibilities, altered dynamics, and redefined priorities, challenging partners with a journey rich with both joy and complexity. On this journey, the essence of partnership is tested and reimagined, as couples grapple

Cultivating and Safeguarding Connection Amidst Life's Transfor... 97

with the demands of nurturing a new life while preserving the sanctity of their bond.

For new parents, the relationship dynamics inevitably undergo a transformation. The once uninterrupted stretches of time for connection and intimacy give way to a schedule dictated by the needs of a newborn. This shift necessitates a recalibration of expectations and a gentle renegotiation of roles that honors the sanctity of the couple's bond while embracing the responsibilities of caregiving. Within this new reality, the strength of the relationship is tested and fortified, as partners learn to grow with grace and resilience. The key to this evolution lies in the ability to communicate openly about the shifting needs and desires, ensuring that both partners feel supported and valued in their new roles.

At the beginning of early parenthood, maintaining the couple's relationship emerges as a paramount concern. It becomes essential to carve out time for connection amidst the challenge of sleepless nights and endless chores. Instituting regular date nights, even if they occur in the living room after the baby has settled, serves as a lifeline to the pre-parenthood self and relationship. These moments, though fleeting, are potent reminders of the love and partnership that form the foundation of the new family. Similarly, nurturing shared interests offers a bridge to mutual fulfillment and joy beyond the realm of parenting, reinforcing the bond that unites the couple in a shared journey of discovery and growth.

Parenthood is a monumental shift, but one of many role changes that couples may face. The prospect of becoming caregivers for aging parents presents another dimension of responsibility that demands adaptability, empathy, and support. This role reversal, with its inherent challenges and emotional weight, requires couples to draw upon the reserves of mutual understanding and resilience cultivated over the course of their relationship. It is a test of the ability to support each other through life's complexities, offer strength when the other falters, and find solace in the shared commitment to care for those who once cared for them. Through this transition, couples learn the value of patience, the strength of empathy, and the depth of their commitment to each other and their extended family.

The essence of a relationship lies in its ability to grow and evolve through the many transitions life presents. Each change, whether the joyous arrival of a child or the somber responsibility of caregiving, offers an opportunity to deepen the connection and understanding between partners. In moving through these transitions together, the relationship is strengthened and the bond deepened in the face of shared challenges and triumphs. This process of continuous growth and adaptation is not merely a response to external circumstances but a conscious choice to evolve together, to turn life's inevitable shifts into avenues for deeper connection and mutual fulfillment.

In embracing life's new roles and responsibilities, couples embark on a journey of mutual discovery, a path marked by challenges but rich with opportunities for growth. The transition to parenthood and beyond, with its profound impact on the relationship, demands a delicate balance of support, communication, and mutual respect. Within this dynamic interplay of roles and responsibilities, the essence of partnership is tested and reaffirmed, offering a testament to the enduring strength and adaptability of love. As couples traverse these transitions, they forge a deeper bond, a connection that is rooted in shared experiences and a commitment to grow together through the seasons of life.

In reflection, the journey through new roles and life's transitions underscores the resilience of partnerships forged in mutual respect, open communication, and shared growth. It is a testament to the enduring power of love to adapt, evolve, and flourish amidst the inevitable changes that life presents. As we turn our gaze forward, we carry with us the lessons learned from these transitions, ready to face the future with confidence in our ability to grow and thrive together, no matter what lies ahead.

Exploring the Impact of Betrayal: Steps Toward Healing

In all human relationships, betrayal stands out as a stark, discordant action, dark against the vibrancy of trust and intimacy. Like a sudden chill on an otherwise warm day, betrayal destroys the equilibrium of a partnership, casting long shadows over the carefully cultivated landscape of love and trust. The act of betrayal, whether through infidelity, deception, or broken promises, acts as a catalyst for profound emotional turmoil, unraveling the fabric of trust that forms the foundation of any relationship.

Understanding the Impact of Betrayal

Psychological and Emotional Effects

Betrayal leaves in its wake a tumultuous range of emotions—hurt, anger, confusion, and disbelief. For the betrayed partner, this emotional maelstrom can manifest as symptoms reminiscent of post-traumatic stress: intrusive thoughts, hyper-vigilance towards the betrayer's actions, and an overwhelming sense of betrayal. The psychological impact extends beyond the immediate emotional reactions, leading to self-doubt and questioning. This disorientation is similar to the confusion experienced when what was once recognizable and comforting becomes strange and uncertain; each memory and shared experience with the partner is now seen through a lens of doubt and unease.

Trust Erosion

Trust, once a solid ground upon which the relationship stood, now resembles a fractured pane of glass—intact yet irrevocably altered. The erosion of this trust affects more than just the perception of the betrayer; it permeates every facet of the relationship, from communication to intimacy. The ease and openness that once characterized conversations give way to hesitance and guardedness, as the betrayed partner grapples with the fear of being wounded anew. Intimacy, too, suffers, as the physical and emotional closeness that once came naturally now feels fraught with doubts and insecurities.

Guilt and Shame in the Betrayer

The betrayer, meanwhile, confronts a tempest of their own—guilt and shame. These emotions, potent and pervasive, can lead to a paradoxical desire to withdraw from the relationship, a reaction driven by the discomfort of facing the pain they've caused. This guilt, if left unaddressed, can act as a barrier to genuine remorse and reparative actions, complicating the healing process. It's a situation reminiscent of a person who, after inadvertently knocking over a vase, is so overwhelmed by guilt that they cannot bring themselves to pick up the pieces, leaving the mess untouched and the relationship in disarray.

Impact on Future Relationships

The reverberations of betrayal extend beyond the confines of the current relationship, casting long shadows on future connections. The betrayed partner may carry into new relationships heavy trust issues, fears, and insecurities, a legacy of the pain they've endured. These issues, if unexamined, can lead to patterns of suspicion and guardedness, affecting the dynamics of new partnerships. It's as though the ghost of betrayal lingers, whispering cautions and doubts, coloring perceptions of trust and fidelity.

In the aftermath of betrayal, understanding its multifaceted impact on both partners and the relationship as a whole is crucial. This comprehension paves the way for a slow and gentle approach to healing, one that acknowledges the depth of the hurt and the complexity of the emotions involved. As couples embark on the delicate process of rebuilding trust, they are guided by the recognition that healing is not a linear path but a journey marked by setbacks and breakthroughs. Through this journey, the potential for growth and deeper connection emerges, illuminated by the lessons learned and the resilience forged in the crucible of betrayal.

Steps to Rebuilding Trust

Acknowledgment of the Betrayal

The journey toward healing begins with the betrayer's acknowledgment of their actions. This crucial first step, though seemingly straightforward, requires a deep and honest confrontation with the truth of their actions and their impact on their partner. It's about more than just admitting to the act; it's a full acceptance of its emotional repercussions, undertaken without defense or denial. This acknowledgment is the foundation for rebuilding trust, signaling a readiness for transparency and accountability. This step demands that the betrayer confront their discomfort head-on, revealing the motivations and misjudgments behind their actions. Only by engaging in this frank and unguarded dialogue with the truth can a foundation be laid for trust to gradually regrow. Though this act cannot reverse what has been done, it manifests a dedication to openness and responsibility, crucial elements in the fragile journey toward reestablishing trust.

Open Communication

With the betrayal laid bare, the relationship is altered, necessitating new methods of communication to work through this unfamiliar new reality. In this context, open communication transcends the mere exchange of words, evolving into a dynamic interplay of listening, understanding, and responding. It's a dialogue characterized by its depth, where words are weighted with the intent to comprehend the full spectrum of the partner's hurt and the betraying partner's remorse. This level of communication fosters a space where emotions are not only voiced but are met with empathy and validation, where each partner's perspective is seen as a vital piece of the healing. This process is a delicate balance of giving and receiving, guided not by a rush to overcome the betrayal, but by the essential need to thoroughly experience every step of recovery. This approach ensures that all underlying issues are addressed and all emotional injuries are carefully healed.

Rebuilding trust is an enduring journey, not a quick fix. It unfolds over time, marked by progress and setbacks alike. Anticipate a path that is non-linear, with moments of advancement and moments of retreat. Adjust your expectations to this reality, understanding that healing from betrayal is not a singular event, but a continuous process that demands patience and commitment from both partners. It's essential to recognize that the relationship, transformed by this process, will not revert to its previous state, but can evolve into something uniquely stronger and more resilient.

Setting New Boundaries

In the aftermath of betrayal, the boundaries that once identified the relationship's safe spaces may be blurred or breached. Restoring or establishing new boundaries is a task that requires both partners' agreement and a profound comprehension of each individual's need for safety and security. These boundaries, however, are not walls meant to distance but guidelines that foster a sense of respect and protection. They are co-created with the flexibility to adapt to the evolving needs of the relationship, filled with the understanding that trust, once fractured, requires clear demarcations of comfort and respect to heal. The process of setting these boundaries is inherently collaborative, a negotiation with the spirit of compromise and the recognition of each partner's vulnerabilities and strengths. Through this collaborative effort, the relationship gains a framework within which trust can be nurtured, offering both partners a sense of agency and reassurance in the journey toward reconciliation.

Rebuilding Through Actions

As the adage goes, actions speak louder than words, a principle that holds profound significance in the context of rebuilding trust. The path to restoration is paved not just with promises or declarations of change but with tangible, consistent actions that demonstrate the betrayer's commitment to the relationship and the healing process. This commitment is manifested in daily acts of transparency, in the deliberate choice to share aspects of one's life that were previously obscured, and in the respect for the new boundaries that have been set. It's visible in the effort to reconnect through shared activities, the patience to rebuild intimacy at a pace that respects the betrayed partner's emotional state, and the unwavering support for the partner's healing, even when the path seems arduous. These actions, repeated day after day, slowly, painstakingly rebuild trust. They serve as evidence of the betrayer's dedication to change and the restoration of the sacred bond of trust that forms the cornerstone of any deep, enduring relationship.

In this difficult and arduous process of rebuilding trust, the relationship undergoes a metamorphosis, emerging from the chrysalis of betrayal and healing with a newfound resilience. The steps outlined above, each demanding its measure of courage and vulnerability, combine to reach renewal, where the scars of betrayal, though never fully erased, become part of a larger narrative of forgiveness, growth, and undiminished hope. Through acknowledgment, open communication, the setting of new boundaries, and the power of actions, the relationship steps into a future where trust, once shattered, finds its form anew, tempered by the trials it has endured and strengthened by the unwavering commitment of both partners to emerge from the shadows of betrayal into the light of understanding and renewed connection.

Navigating the journey of rebuilding trust is inherently complex and unpredictable. As such, couples may encounter moments of significant progress, where small victories highlight the strength and resilience of their bond. However, these moments of triumph are often interspersed with larger setbacks, challenging the patience and resolve of both partners. The essence of true healing lies within the mutual commitment of both individuals. It requires an unwavering dedication to work through the difficulties together, acknowledging each obstacle as an opportunity for growth. Moving forward in unison, with a shared understanding of the challenges ahead, signifies a crucial advancement in the healing process. This shared journey, with its ebbs and flows, underscores the dynamic nature of rebuilding trust—a testament to the power of collective perseverance and the enduring hope for a renewed, stronger connection.

Navigating the Healing Process Together

In the aftermath of betrayal, healing begins with many pathways, each turn promising a step closer to reconciliation and mutual understanding. Devising a mutual healing plan emerges as the key to guiding the couple through the hurt toward renewed connection. Crafting such a plan necessitates a slow, steady interplay of negotiation and compromise, where the steps taken are deliberate and aligned with the pace and rhythm of both partners. It involves delineating clear objectives that address the emotional and practical dimensions of healing, from fostering transparent communication to re-establishing intimacy at a pace that honors the vulnerabilities laid bare by the betrayal. This plan, co-authored with sincerity and foresight, functions as a tangible testament to the couple's dedication to mend the damage wrought by deception, a roadmap that charts the course of their collective journey towards healing.

Throughout this healing journey, empathy is essential, acting as a critical support for the relationship's fragile framework as the partners endeavor to restore the relationship's previous resilience. In this context, empathy goes beyond simple comprehension, extending into the domain of experiencing emotions together. It demands that each partner, for a moment, steps into the other's world, feeling the weight of their pain, the depth of their confusion, and the flickers of hope that persist amidst disillusionment. This profound exchange of perspectives fosters an environment where healing can flourish, rooted in the mutual recognition of each other's humanity and the shared trauma of betrayal. It serves as a reminder that at the heart of the pain lies a bond that, though bruised, retains the capacity for incredible resilience and adaptability.

Healing, however, is fraught with the need for patience, a virtue that becomes both a shield and a salve in the slow process of mending trust. Patience here is not passive; it is an active embrace of the complexity of emotions and setbacks that invariably accompany the journey toward reconciliation. It acknowledges that forgiveness cannot be rushed, that the scars of betrayal, require time to heal and may never fully disappear. This patience is a mutual offering, a gift that each partner bestows upon the other and the relationship, signaling a willingness to weather the storm of healing together. It is an understanding that the path back to trust is winding, marked by moments of progress and periods of stagnation, yet every step taken is a testament to the enduring hope that underpins the decision to heal as a unit.

At the core of this intricate process lies the need to reaffirm commitment to each other and the relationship, a step that serves as both a foundation and a pinnacle in the healing journey. It cannot just be words mouthed by each partner. This reaffirmation must be a powerful act, a declaration that despite the tempest of betrayal, the relationship holds intrinsic value worth fighting for. It involves not just words of assurance but tangible demonstrations of commitment, from dedicating time for shared activities to actively working on strengthening communication and emotional connection. This gesture of reaffirmation guides the relationship through uncertainty, illuminating the enduring love and respect that remains intact amidst the upheaval. It is a mutual pledge to rebuild, to fortify the bonds that have been tested, and to emerge with a relationship that, while irrevocably changed by the experience of betrayal, stands stronger for having navigated the depths of vulnerability and pain together.

Navigating the healing process together through the creation of a healing plan, the exercise of empathy, the cultivation of patience, and the reaffirmation of commitment becomes a transformative experience for the couple. It is a journey that, while born from the ashes of betrayal, offers the opportunity for profound growth, deeper understanding, and a renewed appreciation for the strength and resilience of love. In this shared endeavor, the couple forges a new narrative that acknowledges the scars of the past but looks forward with hope and determination to a future built on the pillars of trust, transparency, and mutual respect.

When to Seek Professional Help

In the chaos and uncertainty of emotions and challenges post-betrayal, discerning when to invite external support into the healing process can be as complex as navigating the healing journey itself. The realization that the relationship may benefit from professional intervention often arrives at a juncture where internal efforts seem insufficient against the weight of unresolved pain and lingering distrust. This acknowledgment is not an admission of defeat but a proactive step towards mending the fractures with expertise that extends beyond the personal realm. Signals necessitating this transition might manifest as recurring disputes over the same issues, a noticeable stagnation in emotional recovery, or an intensifying distance between partners. In these moments, when the path forward becomes obscured by the fog of persistent hurt and misunderstanding, the clarity offered by professional guidance becomes invaluable.

For many dealing with the fallout of betrayal, couples therapy can offer a safe space where feelings can be openly explored and understood in an environment of balanced neutrality. The therapeutic space, characterized by its neutrality, allows for the expression of vulnerabilities and fears without the apprehension of judgment or retaliation. Under the guidance of a seasoned professional, communication barriers are dismantled, facilitating a deeper understanding between partners. The benefits of this therapeutic intervention are manifold, encompassing effective communication strategies, identifying and modifying destructive patterns, and fostering empathy and understanding. This environment encourages transparency and honesty, providing the tools necessary to rebuild a trust foundation. More importantly, it aids in the reconnection of partners as co-navigators of pain and as allies in healing, each committed to the laborious task of weaving trust back into the fabric of their relationship.

For some, the wounds inflicted by betrayal necessitate a more individualized approach to healing. Individual therapy offers a private haven for introspection and growth, allowing the betrayed and the betrayer alike to confront the personal demons that haunt their minds. It serves as a place for the betrayed, in which they can examine the impact of the betrayal on their self-esteem and sense of security, untangling the complex emotions that have taken root. For the betrayer, it presents an opportunity to delve into the motivations behind their actions, exploring the myriad of personal issues that led to the betrayal. This path, though solitary, is instrumental in addressing the internal landscapes marred by the betrayal, facilitating a healing process that is both personal and profound. It offers a chance to rebuild one's sense of self, to emerge from the shadow of betrayal with a clearer understanding of personal values, boundaries, and needs.

Support groups stand as another pillar of external support, offering a collective well of experiences and wisdom for those in the aftermath of betrayal. These groups provide a unique space where stories of pain, resilience, and healing are shared, offering perspectives illuminating the diverse healing pathways. For the betrayed, these narratives affirm that they are not alone in their pain, fostering a sense of solidarity and understanding. For the betrayer, hearing the stories of others who have navigated the thorny path of redemption and reconciliation can be both humbling and enlightening, offering hope and guidance. The communal aspect of support groups engenders a sense of belonging, a balm for the isolation that betrayal often breeds. It's a reminder that the journey of healing, though deeply personal, is also a shared human experience that benefits from the empathy, support, and insight of others who have walked similar paths.

When healing from betrayal, the decision to seek professional help is a pivotal step towards mending the brokenness within oneself and the relationship. Whether through couples therapy, individual therapy, or support groups, this external intervention offers a direction for navigating the complex emotional terrain wrought by betrayal. It provides the tools, strategies, and insights necessary for healing, facilitating a journey that, while fraught with challenges, holds the promise of deeper connection, understanding, and trust. By embracing professional support, couples affirm their commitment to surviving the aftermath of betrayal and thriving beyond it, fortified by the lessons learned and the growth attained through the healing process.

In closing, the journey through betrayal's aftermath and the gradual rebuilding of trust underscores the resilience of the human spirit and the transformative power of love and commitment. Seeking professional help when necessary, engaging in open and empathetic communication, and committing to the healing process underscore the potential for renewal and growth. As we transition from the shadows of betrayal into the light of understanding and forgiveness, we move towards a future where trust, once shattered, finds new strength and where love, tested by adversity, emerges with unimagined depth and resilience. The path ahead, though uncertain, is paved with hope, leading us not back to where we were but forward to where we aspire to be.

Navigating the Tides of Jealousy and Insecurity

Within human connections, jealousy, and insecurity, if left unchecked, can erode even the most robust relationships. These raw and unbridled emotions whisper doubt and fear into the ears of lovers, painting shadows on walls once bathed in the light of trust and intimacy. Yet, within these shadows lie opportunities for growth, for in confronting the specters of jealousy and insecurity, individuals and couples alike can forge stronger, more resilient relationships anchored in understanding and compassion.

Identifying the Roots of Jealousy and Insecurity

Underlying Causes

At the heart of jealousy and insecurity lie deeper, often unspoken fears—fears of abandonment, not being enough, and losing what one holds dear. These emotions do not arise in a vacuum; they are fed by past experiences where trust was damaged, self-esteem that has known doubt, and unmet emotional needs. The initial move in tackling these complex emotions involves identifying and acknowledging their root causes. Just as a gardener needs to know the weeds that threaten their garden to remove them effectively, it's essential for individuals to understand the underlying factors of their jealousy and insecurity to confront and manage these feelings effectively.

Self-Reflection

Self-reflection is a powerful tool in this endeavor, a deliberate turning inward to explore one's heart and mind. In this introspection, one can uncover the triggers of jealousy and insecurity, those specific situations, words, or actions that cause the heart to race and doubt to rise like a tide. Consider the act of journaling, where thoughts and feelings can be poured onto paper and examined in the quiet of solitude. Here, patterns emerge, revealing the outlines of one's fears and desires and offering insights for healing and growth.

Communication Patterns

The ways in which partners communicate—or fail to—can either soothe or exacerbate feelings of jealousy and insecurity. Certain communication habits can spark doubt and fear between partners, including sidestepping challenging conversations, leaving assumptions unexamined, or offering criticism without empathy. Conversely, communication marked by openness, empathy, and a willingness to truly listen and understand can serve as a balm, soothing the pain of insecurity. Strategies to foster positive communication include setting aside dedicated time for conversations, approaching discussions with a mindset of curiosity rather than accusation, and practicing active listening, where the focus is on understanding the partner's perspective rather than formulating a response.

Distinguishing Between Rational and Irrational Jealousy

Not all jealousy is unfounded; herein lies a delicate distinction that requires careful consideration. Rational jealousy, grounded in observable behaviors or situations threatening the relationship, calls for a different response than irrational jealousy, often rooted in personal insecurities and unfounded fears. The key to understanding this distinction lies in evidence and communication. When jealousy arises, taking a step back to objectively assess the situation can provide clarity. When done with openness and a desire for understanding, discussing these feelings with a partner can further illuminate the nature of the jealousy, paving the way for a response that addresses the root of the issue rather than its symptoms.

Interactive Element: Jealousy and Insecurity Self-Assessment Quiz

An interactive self-assessment quiz offers a practical tool for individuals to explore the nature and origins of their feelings of jealousy and insecurity. Through a series of carefully crafted questions, participants can gain insights into their emotional triggers, communication patterns, and the distinction between rational and irrational jealousy. This quiz, accessible online serves as a starting point for deeper reflection and conversation, providing a structured framework for understanding and addressing these complex emotions. See the Chapter 10 references for some very good exercises and worksheets on this topic.

Navigating the complex emotions of jealousy and insecurity can seem daunting. These feelings, deeply rooted in fears and doubts, pose significant challenges. However, by confronting these issues directly, individuals and couples can grow stronger, equipped with greater self-awareness, improved communication skills, and the ability to distinguish between rational and nonsensical. Although uncomfortable, this journey offers an opportunity to foster a deeper understanding and compassion within the relationship, ultimately leading to a more resilient bond in the face of adversity.

Strategies for Overcoming Jealousy in the Relationship

Open and Honest Communication

Sharing one's vulnerabilities without blaming casts starts the journey to mutual understanding. This endeavor involves the risk of exposing one's innermost fears, but it paves the way for authentic dialog. It requires a vocabulary that rejects accusations for introspection. Changing the phrase "You make me feel" into "I feel," is a subtle shift that fosters a space where empathy flourishes. In this environment, partners are encouraged to express their insecurities, framing them not as accusations but as opportunities for closer bonds. Together, they build a narrative where jealousy isn't an isolated battle but a communal challenge to be acknowledged and tackled as a team.

Rebuilding Trust

Rebuilding trust, once damaged by doubt and jealousy, requires careful and patient effort. Each moment must be treated with openness, loyalty, and transparent honesty as a foundational block in restoring faith in one another. This process will not be swift or effortless. It unfolds through the consistency of actions that speak louder than promises of change. Rebuilding trust grows by the willingness to share, to offer unsolicited reassurances, and to make visible the parts of one's life that once remained obscured. Here, demonstrations of trust are not grand gestures but the daily deposits of honesty, the small acts that accumulate into a restored faith in the other. This renewal of trust does not seek to return to a past unmarked by jealousy but to forge ahead to a future where the scars of past hurts inform a stronger, more resilient bond.

Setting Healthy Boundaries

Setting healthy boundaries in a relationship serves as a protective measure and a peaceful haven, marking the areas of personal freedom and mutual respect. These boundaries, established jointly, balance the need for personal space with the desire for closeness. This helps ensure that both partners feel respected and valued without feeling constrained. In this practice, open, loyal, and transparently honest dialogue serves as the compass, guiding the negotiation of boundaries that honor the integrity of both partners, ensuring that the embrace of intimacy does not become a stranglehold of control. Through the process of setting boundaries, both partners feel seen, heard, and valued within the framework of their togetherness.

Focusing on Self-Improvement

Recognizing that jealousy must be acknowledged and addressed is the first step. The next step is looking at self-improvement as a growth avenue, not away from the partner perceived as the source of insecurity but from the internal self-talk that reinforces feelings of inadequacy. Self-enhancement, marked by setting and achieving personal goals and cultivating self-esteem, begins to offer peace and solace from comparison and doubt. It demands courage, for in gazing inward, one must confront the memories of insecurity that speak of not being enough. Yet, in this internal confrontation, growth begins as individuals learn to understand that their sense of worth is not from the external validation of their partner but from their accomplishments and virtues. Pursuing personal interests, self-care dedication, and personal development commitment is a growth path. Each step moves toward a self that is more whole, more secure, and less dependent on another's appraisal for its sense of value. In this growth, jealousy has less power, not because the triggers have vanished but because the individual has evolved beyond its reach.

The strategies outlined above offer a multifaceted approach to understanding, addressing, and transcending this challenging emotion. Through open, loyal, and transparently honest communication, rebuilding trust, setting healthy boundaries, and a focus on self-improvement, couples can transform the poison of jealousy into the medicine of deeper connection and self-awareness. This shift in perspective does not dismiss the discomfort or intricacies inherent in feelings of jealousy but recognizes their potential to spark significant personal and mutual development. Seen through this lens, jealousy is recast not as a foe to be defeated but as an instructor, leading partners to more profound and genuine expressions of love and togetherness.

Building Self-Esteem and Trust Within

Enhancing self-worth is much like tending to an inner garden, where recognizing and valuing personal virtues and strengths helps grow confidence and resilience. This internal space, often cluttered with self-criticism and self-doubt, demands careful nurturing to thrive. Recognizing and celebrating one's inherent qualities and achievements is not merely an act of vanity. Instead, it is a profound exercise in self-discovery and appreciation. One must pause for a moment of introspection, where one sifts through the layers of external expectations and societal norms to uncover the firm foundation of one's true self. Being disciplined and taking the steps of introspection, such as listing achievements, however small, or identifying moments of courage and kindness, reflects the multifaceted beauty of one's character and capabilities.

This evolves with each new realization, creating a collage of the individual that is both grounded in reality and inspirational in its scope.

Self-compassion becomes a soothing balm for the scars of negative self-talk and harsh self-judgment. It demands as much unlearning as learning, a paradigm from self-criticism to kindness and understanding. Extending the same compassion to oneself that one would to a dear friend requires breaking down the inner dialog of unworthiness and self-reproach that stand in the way of self-acceptance. Techniques rooted in mindfulness, such as guided meditations focused on self-compassion or journaling exercises that reframe negative thoughts, offer practical pathways toward cultivating a gentle, forgiving relationship with oneself. This practice is difficult and requires commitment and discipline to change the cycle of self-criticism and create a sense of peace and contentment.

Independence, which includes the physical, intellectual, and emotional areas of one's life, is a cornerstone for building trust in one's abilities and decisions. While pursuing personal interests and passions may seem a solitary and perhaps selfish choice, it is an act of profound self-care that should be available to each partner. Through these activities, artistic, academic, physical and athletic, or ventures into the unknown, individuals discover the depths of their resilience, creativity, and strength. Becoming independent is a journey and it is marked by moments of triumph and tribulation. Each of these is evidence of the individual's capacity to navigate the complexities of life with agency and autonomy. It grows a sense of self-efficacy, the belief in one's ability to effect change in one's life and environment, and that, in turn, reinforces the foundation of self-esteem and trust within.

The path to growing and improving self-esteem and a solid trust in oneself sometimes requires the guidance of someone outside one's own experience. Professional support can help accelerate the journey of self-discovery and healing. Therapists and counselors, with their expertise and experience, can offer insights and strategies to each individual's unique emotional reality. They can help people see patterns of thought and behavior that may not be easily visible to the individual and can hinder the growth of self-esteem. This professional intervention is proof of an individual's commitment to their well-being and growth. It provides a safe space for internal exploration and understanding of oneself and their capacity for change. Support from a professional, along with the individual's commitment and motivation, creates a powerful team to assist personal growth, grow self-esteem, and build inner trust.

This is a deeply personal process. Yet, it reinforces the universal desire to be accepted and understood, which, in turn, reflects humanity's desire for validation and empathy. By recognizing personal strengths, practicing self-compassion, pursuing independence, and, when necessary, reaching out for professional support, individuals embark on a transformative process. This path, characterized by deep self-reflection, continuous learning, and consistent personal development, culminates in the revelation of an inner self that is both strong and flexible, deserving of love and respect from oneself.

Creating Boundaries Around External Influences

Within modern relationships, external influences, digital or personal, force themselves into the private place of love and trust shared by two individuals. Social media platforms, constantly on, constantly bombarding us with the allegedly perfect lives of our friends, act as windows (and sometimes magnifying glasses) into the lives of others. It can introduce a complex layer of visibility and comparison, which, if taken at face value, can create jealousy and insecurity about the wonderful lives of others. But the reality is so much different. No one's life is so marvelous that every selfie is immediately ready to post to Instagram or Facebook. Only the most perfect pictures make it to social media, loudly announcing to the world, "Look how incredible I am," while masking the pain, hurt, and longing that all of us feel. There are only two true methods to manage and mitigate the intrusion of social media. The first is to realize and accept that no one on social media is truly honest with their posts and pictures. The second is to rigorously control the amount of time spent on those platforms. Additionally, partners must be in agreement with what is shared of the relationship. What to share, with whom to share, and with whom to privately chat must be decided between both partners, each committing to the limits and boundaries.

Furthermore, external flirtations present a peculiar challenge, stirring up insecurity and jealousy with its implied threats to the relationship's exclusivity. Here, the role of open dialogue, underscored by a commitment to honesty and vulnerability, cannot be overstated. When situations arise where one partner feels the sting of jealousy due to external attention directed toward the other, navigating these choppy waters requires a delicate balance of reaffirming commitment to each other while addressing the underlying insecurities that such situations unearth. Rejecting flirtatious advances is important. Any person who would jeopardize a relationship by trying to win the affection of a partner in a committed relationship has no respect for the existing relationship. Mutual respect is key to keeping the relationship steady, ensuring both partners feel valued and heard, and minimizing the turbulence caused by external flirtations.

The influence of friends and family on the relationship's dynamics creates another layer of complexity. These connections can either bolster the relationship or unwittingly undermine it, depending on the boundaries set by the couple. Collaboratively, the partners must establish the rules for interactions with friends and family. The intent isn't to limit or exclude but to create parameters within which the partnership can thrive. Within this context, the relationship's autonomy must be fiercely guarded and articulated; decisions made within the partnership need to stand resilient against the well-meaning but potentially divisive opinions of external parties. Cultivating a private space where the couple can grow, unencumbered by external expectations and pressures, is crucial to protecting the relationship.

Finally, maintaining a united front in the face of external influences that challenge the relationship's security demonstrates the solidarity and cohesion of the partnership. This unity, however, is not born of a denial of individual perspectives but from a deep, mutual understanding and a commitment to presenting a cohesive stance to the world. The relationship strengthens against the erosive forces of jealousy and insecurity in this shared solidity. It is a fortress built on the bedrock of mutual trust, respect, and the unyielding support of one partner for the other.

To conclude, the essence of working through jealousy and insecurity within the sphere of love and partnership crystallizes into a few core tenets: the cultivation of open, honest communication; the deliberate setting and respecting of boundaries, both digital and personal; the nurturing of self-esteem and trust within each individual; and the vigilant maintenance of unity in the face of external pressures and influences. These strategies fortify the bonds between partners, transforming potential vulnerabilities into strengths. In this fortified space, the relationship thrives, resilient against the incursions of jealousy and insecurity, enriched by the challenges it has weathered. As we turn our gaze forward, away from the shadows cast by jealousy and insecurity, we see the light of understanding, empathy, and a deeper, more profound connection.

Cultivating Mutual Respect and Appreciation

Appreciation emerges as a significant element in our relationships. It may not capture the immediate attention like the vivid colors of love and passion, but its role is crucial in enhancing the overall harmony and beauty of the relationship. With its gentle impact, it can transform the ordinary into the extraordinary. In this context, genuine appreciation becomes not just an act of acknowledgment but a transformative force capable of deepening connections and elevating the quality of the relationship itself.

The Power of Appreciation in Relationships

The notion that expressing appreciation can significantly elevate relationship satisfaction is hardly novel, yet acting on this idea in the daily grind of life can be challenging. In moments shared over morning coffee, where a simple "thank you for making this" can turn an ordinary routine into a cherished ritual, the power of appreciation manifests. In these small exchanges, the foundation of a positive environment is laid, fostering a culture of gratitude that enriches both partners emotionally.

Turning towards the seemingly mundane, the importance of noticing and acknowledging small acts of kindness and effort becomes apparent. Picture a scenario where one partner decides to tidy up the living space after a long day, an act unnoticed. A subsequent acknowledgment, perhaps over dinner, not only highlights the effort made but also reinforces the value of the gesture. That acknowledgment contributes to an atmosphere of mutual respect and appreciation. This conscious effort to recognize the contributions of the other, no matter how minor they may seem, eases the wear and tear of daily life, strengthening the emotional bond between partners.

Consistent expressions of appreciation, without any ulterior motive or expectation of reciprocity, create a stronger emotional connection. It's similar to watering a plant. Regular nourishment leads to growth and blossoming, transforming the relationship into a vibrant ecosystem of mutual support and understanding. This sincerity of expression distinguishes genuine appreciation from flattery; the former is rooted in deep recognition of the other's value, while the latter often serves as a superficial, self-serving gesture.

Amid the complex rhythms of a relationship, where emotions and connections ebb and flow, the act of appreciation emerges as a cornerstone. It acts as an anchor and a beacon, nurturing mutual respect and admiration that forms a resilient foundation, allowing love and intimacy to deepen. Simultaneously, it guides partners toward a deeper understanding and connection, allowing them to gracefully navigate life's challenges. In this light, appreciation transcends mere emotional expression to become vital to a thriving and enduring relationship.

Recognizing and Valuing Differences

In a partnership, life is marked by the rhythm of individuality, where each beat echoes the distinct melodies of personal history, beliefs, and dreams. In this space, relationships thrive not on uniformity but through the harmony of differences. Celebrating individuality within a relationship does not merely entail acknowledging differences; it involves a deep appreciation for how these variances create a shared life. This celebration transforms what might be perceived as discord into a rich, complex harmony that adds depth and texture to the relationship. Imagine, for a moment, a world painted in a single color—it is through the contrast and diversity of hues that beauty and depth are truly appreciated. Similarly, it is the differences within each partner that enriches the relationship and partner's shared existence.

This appreciation is paved with the understanding that agreement is not the cornerstone of a robust relationship, but rather, understanding is. To gaze into the heart of one's partner, to see the world through their eyes without the compulsion to redirect their gaze, is an act of profound respect and love. It requires an openness to explore their convictions with curiosity, rather than the intent to colonize. This distinction between understanding and agreement is subtle yet significant; it acknowledges that love does not demand conformity, but flourishes with mutual respect. Each conversation, then, becomes not a battleground for supremacy of opinion but a bridge that connects two worlds.

As partners learn from each other, differences reveal themselves not as chasms that divide, but as gateways to new worlds of thought and experience. Each variance in perspective or preference becomes an invitation to expand one's own worldview, to step beyond the familiar into the exhilarating unknown. This expansion is not a passive process; it demands active engagement, a willingness to question and be questioned, to explore and be explored. Navigating through the diversity of each other's personalities and backgrounds is like embarking on a voyage across uncharted seas. Each difference encountered steers the couple towards new discoveries about themselves and each other, lending a dynamic and ever-evolving quality to their relationship. This process of continuous exploration prevents the relationship from becoming stagnant, ensuring that it grows and deepens over time.

Relationships weave together strands from diverse cultural and personal backgrounds, each strand unique in its origins. Navigating these differences requires more than mere tolerance; it necessitates a genuine respect and integration of these diverse experiences into the fabric of the relationship. Strategies to bridge these variances range from the simple act of sharing and celebrating cultural traditions to the more complex process of understanding and negotiating the influence of background differences on relationship dynamics. This integration does not mean the erasure of individual backgrounds in favor of a homogenized middle ground; rather, it involves creating a new, shared space where the richness of each culture and background is preserved and celebrated. It is a delicate balance to strike, requiring constant communication, negotiation, and, above all, a deep respect for the other's heritage as integral to their identity.

In this landscape of differences, the relationship becomes a microcosm of the broader world, a space where diversity is not merely acknowledged but revered as the source of its strength and beauty. It is a testament to the fact that love, in its truest form, is not a force of assimilation but one of profound acceptance.

Daily Habits to Show Respect and Appreciation

In everyday life, routines shape the backdrop of our experiences. Incorporating small acts of gratitude and appreciation can elevate the ordinary into a celebration of mutual respect and admiration. Incorporating gratitude into our daily routines works like magic, turning simple moments into special ones that lift our spirits and strengthen our connection. It's similar to nurturing a beloved garden; you need to be aware of the small changes in your interactions and ready to plant seeds of appreciation daily.

The manifestation of this gratitude does not need to be grandiose. Its power lies in the authenticity of its expression. A note left on the pillow before departing for work, a message midday simply to share a moment of beauty or humor, the preparation of a meal with the partner's preferences in mind—each act, small in itself, becomes a testament to the consideration and thoughtfulness that underpin the relationship. These tokens of appreciation, woven into the fabric of daily routines, are constant reminders of the value placed on the partnership and each other's presence in one's life.

Simultaneously, cultivating respectful communication is a cornerstone in the edifice of a healthy relationship. It is not merely avoiding harsh words or tempering criticism but a deeper, more nuanced endeavor. It involves the active engagement of listening, not just to respond but to understand and to fully immerse oneself in the perspective of the other. This kind of communication demands mindfulness in language use, where words are chosen not for their efficiency but for their ability to convey respect and empathy. Thoughtful responses become not just replies but bridges, connecting hearts and minds in a shared understanding that transcends the spoken word.

Additionally, touch has a special role in conveying love and appreciation. Physical signs of affection, whether through a gentle hand squeeze or a comforting hug, speak volumes beyond words. They accentuate our daily interactions, serving as symbols of joy in happy moments, offering pauses for breath during stressful times and marking the end of a day together. These simple yet profound gestures express an appreciation that words alone cannot fully capture, wrapping your partner in a physical manifestation of love and respect.

In this age of constant motion and distraction, offering quality time emerges as perhaps the most eloquent expression of appreciation. To dedicate one's undivided attention to the partner, to set aside the myriad demands of the external world, to turn off your devices and inhabit a shared space of presence, is to honor the relationship with the gift of oneself. This time, whether spent in shared activity or comfortable silence, becomes a sanctuary, a respite from the cacophony of the outside world where the relationship is nurtured and cherished. In these moments, stripped of pretense and distraction, the true essence of the partnership is revealed and celebrated, a reminder of the unique connection that thrives between the two.

Within a relationship, these daily acts of respect and appreciation create a brilliant mosaic filled with the hues of affection, comprehension, and reciprocal esteem. They act as gentle yet consistent reminders of the splendor found in the shared voyage, a splendor that is nurtured with every considerate word, each soft caress, and every instance of focused attention offered with generosity and affection. Through these actions, a relationship transforms from merely a symbol of love's durability to an active, dynamic presence that grows and prospers under the nurturing glow of shared admiration and regard.

Overcoming Taken-for-Granted Syndrome

Within long-term relationships, the potential for complacency often lurks, its presence subtly eroding the vibrancy of connection that once thrived on the novelty of discovery and the zeal of new affection. This phenomenon, colloquially termed the Taken-for-Granted Syndrome, manifests silently, its symptoms not always immediately apparent but deeply felt. Couples may find themselves ensnared in routines that, while comfortable, lack the spark of earlier days, where expressions of gratitude and acts of kindness become rarities rather than the norm. The first step toward rekindling the dimmed light of appreciation lies in the keen observation of these signs of complacency—unenthusiastic greetings, infrequent expressions of gratitude, or the absence of spontaneous acts of kindness. Recognizing these indicators is, in reality, diagnosing the relationship's health, providing a clear signal that intervention is necessary to revive the warmth that has cooled under the weight of the routine.

Re-igniting thoughtfulness and consideration requires more than the mere intention to do better; it demands actionable strategies that transform good intentions into tangible expressions of affection and regard. One approach involves creating opportunities to surprise and delight one another, such as reintroducing the element of unpredictability that characterizes the early stages of romance. This could manifest in unexpected gestures—leaving a note in a partner's bag or planning a surprise outing to a place with special meaning. These acts, infused with personal significance, serve as powerful antidotes to the creeping malaise of complacency, reawakening the sense of being treasured that is fundamental to a fulfilling partnership.

Cultivating a culture of mutual appreciation within the relationship transcends the mere avoidance of taking each other for granted; it requires the active construction of an environment where gratitude is not just expressed but woven into the fabric of daily interactions. This culture is characterized by the persistent vocalization of appreciation for both the mundane and the significant, ensuring that no act of kindness or support goes unrecognized. It's a practice that demands mindfulness, an ongoing awareness of how each partner contributes to the other's happiness and well-being. By fostering this culture, couples can transform their relationship into a wellspring of positivity, where each partner feels valued for what they do and who they are.

Institutionalizing regular appreciation check-ins can serve as a structural reinforcement of this culture, providing a dedicated space and time for partners to articulate and acknowledge the ways in which they feel seen and appreciated. These check-ins, whether conducted over a quiet dinner at home or during a reflective moment on a weekend morning, offer a pause from the rush of life, a temporal oasis where the focus shifts from the external to the internal, from tasks to feelings. It's an opportunity for partners to share their gratitude and their needs and desires, fostering a deeper connection continually refreshed by the waters of open communication and mutual respect.

As this chapter on cultivating mutual respect and appreciation draws to a close, we are reminded of gratitude's transformative power in relationships and life. The journey from recognizing the signs of complacency to actively countering them with thoughtfulness, consideration, and establishing a culture of appreciation is both challenging and rewarding. It requires a commitment to cherishing the partner and the bond that unites, ensuring that it remains vibrant, resilient, and deeply satisfying. As we move forward, let us carry with us the understanding that appreciation, in its many forms, is the lifeblood of love, nourishing and sustaining it through the seasons of life.

Planning Together for the Adventure of Tomorrow

In our daily routines, the personal journeys we pursue and the joint dreams we aim to realize come together, forming a vibrant mosaic filled with hope, ambition, and mutual respect. This intricate interplay of supporting individual development while building a shared future is crucial for a strong relationship. It resembles two artists in front of a canvas, each holding their palette of colors, not only choosing the image they want to create but also agreeing on the techniques and themes that will shape their artwork.

Setting Shared Goals and Dreams

Identifying Common Values and Goals

A foundation built on shared values and goals is at the core of every enduring partnership. Like two climbers tethered together, navigating the ascent of a mountain, the strength of their bond and the success of their journey rely heavily on their shared commitment to a common path. This alignment does not negate their individual routes or the personal peaks they aim to conquer; rather, it ensures that their journey is marked by mutual support and a deep understanding of their collective end goal.

To navigate this process, couples might sit down with a map of their aspirations, marking not just the peaks they wish to summit but also the valleys of their fears and the rivers of their hopes that meander through the landscape of their future. This exercise, perhaps undertaken during a long weekend, transforms into a ritual of connection, a time to reflect on the essence of their partnership and the dreams that pulse at its heart.

Creating a Vision for the Future

Building a shared vision for the future can be likened to cultivating a garden as a couple. Each dream or goal is like to a seed, chosen with intention and tended with dedication, recognizing that while some dreams may flourish swiftly, others may require more time to mature. This metaphorical garden symbolizes their united aspirations, a collaborative endeavor that demands patience, attentiveness, and the flexibility to adjust to evolving conditions.

An effective tool in this creative process is a vision board, a collage of images, quotes, and symbols representing the couple's dreams and aspirations. This visual element serves as a daily reminder of their shared goals, a beacon that guides their decisions and actions, ensuring they remain aligned with their desired future.

The Importance of Flexibility

Flexibility in planning for the future is not just a strategy but a necessity. It acknowledges that life, in its infinite complexity, often unfolds in ways that defy our expectations. Like a tree that bends in the wind, couples that embrace flexibility in their planning are more likely to withstand the storms of change, adapting their paths while remaining rooted in their shared values and goals.

This adaptability can be fostered through regular check-ins, moments set aside to assess the progress towards their goals and to recalibrate their plans in response to the inevitable shifts in their circumstances. These discussions, held perhaps over a shared meal or during a walk, become sacred spaces for reflection, adjustment, and recommitment to their shared journey.

Documenting and Revisiting Goals

The act of documenting shared goals serves as both a testament to a couple's commitment and a roadmap for their future. Whether inscribed in a shared journal, plotted on a digital platform, or embodied in a collaborative art piece, these records are milestones, marking the path they have chosen to walk together. This chapter unravels the intricate process of planning together for the future

A helpful method that gives goals power and traction is to make them SMART goals. SMART is an acronym that means:

S - Specific - This speaks to being precise with the goal. A simple example would be saving money. A person could have as a goal, "I want to save more money." Pretty generic. How much is "more" money? Ten dollars? Twenty? Specific would be saying, "I want to save $2400."

M - Measurable - Continuing our example, more is not very specific and can't be measured. Any money saved could meet that criteria. But being specific about how much, $2400, gives a person something they can measure against.

A - Achievable - This aspect is important, but a person shouldn't always settle for easy. Again, using our example, maybe $2400 could be saved in a week. Or perhaps it would take 19 years. The specific detail should be challenging to engage our motivation but not so extreme as to be unachievable. For many of us, saving a million dollars in a year is not going to happen regardless of what we do. For others, it is achievable. Stretch yourself, but don't discourage yourself.

R - Realistic - The goal should be realistic. A person could say they want to save $2400, but if they want to save it in the next 15 minutes, well for most of us, that isn't going to happen. Or, a different example, a person could say, "I want my college degree in hand this year." but they haven't even taken a single class. Not realistic.

T - Timebound - Finally, timebound is the last aspect that keeps people focused and engaged in their goals. Set a specific time to achieve the goal. Don't be unrealistic, but as with achievable, but make the process take effort. Do the math in the saving money example. "If I save $200 each month, I will achieve my goal by December 31." As the weeks and months pass by, a person can see how they are progressing against the goal. If they are falling behind, they can press harder. If they are ahead, they can hit the goal early, and set another one.

The intention of the SMART goal is to create something that keeps people engaged and active in pursuing it. It is critical to write it down. Unwritten goals are the weakest of goals and are not usually met.

Equally important is the practice of revisiting these goals, a ritual that allows couples to celebrate their achievements, acknowledge their challenges, and renew their commitment to their shared vision. This practice, embedded in the rhythm of their lives, ensures that their goals remain relevant and responsive to the evolving landscape of their relationship.

In this chapter, the intricate process of planning together for the future is unraveled, revealing not just the strategies and tools that can guide couples on this path but also the profound significance of this shared endeavor. It highlights how the act of setting, pursuing, and revisiting shared goals and dreams is not just a logistical exercise but a profound expression of love, trust, and mutual respect. Through this collaborative journey, couples not only shape their future but also deepen their connection, weaving a tapestry of shared experiences, aspirations, and achievements that enriches the fabric of their relationship.

Navigating Differences in Future Aspirations

In the delicate balance of partnership, individual desires, and shared goals intertwine, creating a rich tapestry that showcases unity and distinctiveness. The skill in harmonizing personal goals with joint aims is nuanced and significant. It requires profound respect for each partner's aspirations, acknowledging that the relationship's fabric becomes stronger, not weaker, when partners support each other's personal endeavors. This shared understanding forms the foundation for crafting approaches to bridge divergent ambitions, ensuring the partnership's tapestry remains dynamic and enhanced by the variety of its patterns.

Communicating About Divergent Goals

The dialogue that unfolds between partners about their individual paths is a dance of words and silences, of speaking and listening, that requires both grace and intention. Effective communication in this context is less about persuasion and more about revelation, a gentle unveiling of the dreams that pulse within each heart. It involves not only the articulation of one's aspirations but also an attentive, open-hearted listening to the other's. Such conversations are textured with vulnerability, a willingness to lay bare one's dreams, however nascent or audacious they may seem. They are punctuated by questions that seek to clarify, not challenge, by reflections that mirror understanding, and by responses that validate, even when they do not align. This dialogue becomes the loom on which the future is woven, a future that honors both the individual and the shared, the singular and the plural.

Finding Common Ground

The search for common ground amidst divergent aspirations is much like charting a course through a landscape rich with both harmony and discord. It requires a map drawn not in rigid lines but in fluid strokes that allow for detours and new discoveries. Techniques for uncovering this common ground might involve identifying intersections between seemingly disparate goals or finding shared values that underlie different aspirations. It might mean creating a new dream, one that encompasses elements of each partner's vision, or alternating focus, dedicating time and resources to support each dream in turn. This process is iterative, a continual process that respects the dynamic nature of individual growth and relationship evolution. It acknowledges that common ground is not a static destination but a fertile field, constantly tilled and tended, where new seeds of shared dreams can be sown and nurtured.

Supporting Each Other's Individual Goals

The strength of a partnership is often measured by its capacity to support the flourishing of each individual within it. This support is a multifaceted gem, reflecting not just encouragement but also practical assistance, not just cheerleading but also constructive feedback. It is rooted in the belief that fulfilling one's partner's dreams adds, rather than detracts, from the richness of the shared life. Supporting each other's goals involves verbal affirmation and actions demonstrating commitment to the other's success. It might mean stepping in to shoulder more household responsibilities so the other can pursue further education, or it might involve financial sacrifice to invest in a partner's entrepreneurial venture. This support is not transactional but transformational, a tangible manifestation of love that empowers each to reach for their highest potential.

Balancing Individual and Shared Aspirations

The equilibrium between individual and shared aspirations is a dynamic balance, constantly adjusted to accommodate the shifting weights of personal growth and collective endeavor. It is an equilibrium that is not imposed but co-created, forged through ongoing dialogue, mutual support, and the shared crafting of a future that is both deeply fulfilling and joyously communal. Balancing these aspirations requires a keen awareness of the rhythms of the relationship, an attunement to when to push forward with joint projects and when to create space for individual pursuits. It involves a mutual generosity of spirit, a rejoicing in the other's achievements as if they were one's own, and a commitment to weaving together a life that celebrates both togetherness and autonomy.

In this complex process of balancing differing journeys, the relationship transforms into a fertile ground for growth, a realm where dreams are not merely exchanged but also sculpted and refined by the truths of companionship and external challenges. It is here, in the delicate interplay of difference, that the true art of partnership is revealed, an art marked by deep respect, unwavering support, and the joyful creation of a shared future that is vibrant with the colors of individual dreams and collective aspirations.

The Role of Compromise in Future Planning

Within relationships, compromise doesn't signify a loss but rather unfolds as a graceful step toward mutual satisfaction and insight. This nuanced interaction, often misconceived as relinquishing one's desires for the sake of peace, is, in truth, a potent force—a testament to the strength and resilience inherent in the decision to intertwine lives and dreams. To compromise is to sculpt from the raw material of individual aspirations a shared future that resonates with the depth and complexity of the bond itself. Within this context, the act of finding middle ground is elevated from mere negotiation to an art form, a delicate balance of give and take that enriches rather than diminishes the individual and collective journey.

Compromise as a Strength

To reframe compromise as a strength requires a shift in perspective, a recognition that the ability to blend desires and needs is not a sign of weakness but a robust marker of a relationship's capacity to evolve and adapt. This strength is born from the understanding that in the vast landscape of a shared life, the territories of the self and the other are not rigidly demarcated but fluid, their borders constantly reshaped by the ebb and flow of experience, growth, and understanding. It is in the willingness to navigate these shifting terrains together, to occasionally step back so the other might step forward, that the true fortitude of the partnership is revealed. This dynamic interplay, far from diminishing the individual, amplifies the breadth of possibilities available to both, crafting from the multitude of paths a journey that is richer for its shared direction.

Practical Compromise Strategies

The architecture of compromise is constructed on foundations of transparency, empathy, and an unwavering commitment to the health of the relationship. Strategies for reaching compromises that honor both partners' needs and desires are manifold, each tailored to the unique contours of the partnership. One approach involves the creation of a shared decision-making space, a neutral ground where aspirations can be laid bare without the shadow of judgment, and each partner's voice is given equal weight. Within this space, active listening becomes a tool of unparalleled power, a means through which to understand not just the surface request but the deeper need that fuels it. Another strategy employs the use of "if-then" scenarios, a method that allows for the exploration of outcomes and the mutual shaping of a path forward. This collaborative problem-solving approach ensures that compromises are not just accepted but co-created, a reflection of shared values and mutual respect.

Avoiding Resentment

The shadows that compromise can cast are often tinged with the hues of resentment, a corrosive element that has the potential to undermine the very foundation it seeks to strengthen. Avoiding this pitfall requires vigilance and a commitment to open channels of communication. It necessitates a regular re-engagement with the terms of the compromise, a willingness to revisit and, if necessary, recalibrate in response to the shifting dynamics of the relationship and the individuals within it. Key to this process is the practice of expressing needs and feelings continuously, not as a flood but as a steady stream, ensuring that small grievances are addressed before they swell into rivers of discontent. Equally important is the cultivation of a personal practice of reflection, an internal dialogue through which to process feelings of sacrifice or loss, allowing them to be seen, acknowledged, and, ultimately, released.

Celebrating Compromises

In the celebration of compromises, couples find not just a moment of acknowledgment but a profound reaffirmation of their commitment to the collective over the individual, to the 'us' that encompasses and transcends the 'me' and 'you.' These celebrations, whether marked by a simple gesture of gratitude or a more elaborate ritual of acknowledgment, serve as milestones, reminders of the journey traversed together and the shared victories won. They imbue the act of compromise with a sense of joy, transforming what might be perceived as a surrender of individual desires into a celebration of mutual growth and understanding. In this light, compromises become not just a necessary component of future planning but a cherished aspect of the relationship's narrative, a story of love's capacity to bridge divides and forge from them a stronger, more resilient bond.

Celebrating Milestones and Creating New Traditions

In the shared journey of a relationship, recognizing milestones acts as a vibrant thread, celebrating the path taken while enriching the relationship's tapestry with extraordinary depth. These milestones, be they anniversaries of togetherness, achievements in personal or professional realms, or simply moments that hold a special place in the heart of the partnership, are beacons that illuminate the path traversed, casting a light that both warms and guides. It is through these celebrations that couples anchor their experiences in the realm of the cherished, transforming fleeting moments into enduring memories that weave through the narrative of their shared existence.

The creation of new traditions, in this context, emerges as a dynamic expression of the couple's evolving identity. These traditions, born from the unique alchemy of their combined spirits, serve not just as rituals to mark the passage of time but as living embodiments of their shared values and dreams. They are acts of creation that reflect the couple's journey, echoing the laughter, tears, and triumphs that define their story. Whether it's the simple act of preparing a meal together to celebrate the end of a week, taking an annual trip to a place that holds special meaning, or dedicating an evening to reflect on the highs and lows of the year, these traditions become the milestones of tomorrow, markers of growth and joy in the ever-unfolding story of their lives.

Reflecting on growth and achievements, then, becomes an integral part of this narrative. It is a practice that transcends mere reminiscence, inviting a deeper exploration of the ways in which each partner, and the relationship itself, has evolved. This reflection is both a mirror and a window—a mirror reflecting the journey thus far, with all its challenges and triumphs, and a window opening to the possibilities that lie ahead. It is an opportunity to pause, to breathe in the essence of the journey shared, and to recognize the ways in which individual growth has contributed to the flourishing of the relationship. This practice of reflection not only reinforces the bond but also renews the spirit, infusing the partnership with a sense of purpose and direction.

Renewing commitment, as a culmination of this reflective process, becomes a sacred act of affirmation. It is a declaration, spoken in the quiet spaces between heartbeats, that the journey shared is not merely to be continued but to be deepened. This renewal of commitment might manifest in a myriad of ways—a vow renewal ceremony, a quiet affirmation shared in the privacy of a shared space, or a collaborative project that symbolizes their united vision for the future. It is an acknowledgment that, while the path may twist and turn, the decision to walk it together remains steadfast. This act of renewal serves as a bridge between the chapters of their story, a pledge to navigate the waters of the future with the same courage, love, and dedication that has marked their journey thus far.

In the realm of love and partnership, the celebration of milestones and the creation of new traditions are acts of profound significance. They serve as testaments to the journey shared, to the growth achieved, and to the enduring commitment that forms the bedrock of the relationship. Through these acts, couples not only honor the past but also lay the foundation for the future, weaving a tapestry that is vibrant with the colors of their shared experiences, dreams, and aspirations. It is in these moments of celebration and reflection that the essence of the partnership is both captured and released, a reminder that the journey shared is one of continual discovery, renewal, and deepening connection.

As we move forward, the tapestry that unfolds is one that is ever enriched by the love, dedication, and shared vision that define the heart of the relationship. It is a tapestry that, in its complexity and beauty, serves as a living testament to the power of two hearts united in a common purpose, navigating the unfolding chapters of their shared story with grace, resilience, and an unwavering commitment to each other.

Conclusion

As we draw to the end of this journey together, I hope you feel invigorated and inspired by the transformational path we've embarked upon. From the foundational stones of active listening and expressing needs without conflict to the strategies for navigating life's inevitable ups and downs, this book has aimed to guide you toward a deeper understanding, connection, and growth within your relationship. The journey of applying these principles and exercises is one of continuous discovery and evolution, reflecting the dynamic nature of love itself.

We've traversed a landscape rich with opportunities for strengthening communication, resolving disagreements constructively, and deepening emotional as well as physical intimacy. Together, we've explored the importance of managing financial stress collaboratively and supporting each other through significant life transitions. The roadmap provided for healing after betrayal, underscored by insights from experts, has aimed to offer solace and actionable steps towards rebuilding trust. And finally, our discussions on planning for a shared future have highlighted the beauty of weaving individual dreams into a collective tapestry of aspirations.

The universality and adaptability of the advice within these pages are its cornerstone, designed to resonate with all couples, regardless of where you are in your journey together, your financial landscape, or cultural background. This book stands on the robust shoulders of research and insights from renowned psychologists, therapists, and researchers, offering you not just theories but tested strategies for nurturing a resilient and fulfilling partnership.

I urge you not to view this book as a one-time read but as a companion in your ongoing journey of growth and improvement. Revisit the exercises, reflect on the principles shared, and continuously weave the communication and conflict resolution techniques into the fabric of your daily lives. Remember, the path to a meaningful and enduring partnership is paved with mutual effort, understanding, and commitment.

Despite the hurdles and challenges that relationships inevitably face, I want to leave you with a message of hope. Lasting love and deep connection are not just ideals; they are attainable realities for those who dare to dream and work toward them. Your commitment to each other, fueled by the strategies and insights shared, can cultivate a partnership that not only endures but flourishes.

In closing, I want to express my deepest gratitude for allowing me to be a part of your relationship journey. Your dedication to fostering a more understanding, intimate, and resilient bond with your partner is a testament to the power of love and commitment. May this book serve as a beacon of hope, guiding you towards a future filled with joy, understanding, and an unbreakable connection. Here's to the journey ahead, filled with love, growth, and endless possibilities.

Warmly,

Riley

Keeping the Love Alive

Now that you have everything you need to deepen and improve your relationships, it's time to pass on your newfound knowledge and show other readers where they can find the same help.

Remember how it felt when you first started reading The Complete Relationship Guide for Couples? Maybe you were looking for answers, support, or just a little advice. Now think about how much you've learned and how much stronger your relationship has become. It's pretty amazing, right?

Imagine someone else out there, just like you were, searching for guidance. They could be feeling lost or unsure about how to make their relationship better. Your review could be the beacon of hope they need to take the first step.

By sharing your thoughts, you can:

...help another couple communicate better.
...bring more love and understanding into someone's home.
...make a real difference in someone's life.

It only takes a minute, but your review can have a lasting impact. So, why not take that moment to help someone else on their journey to a happier, healthier relationship?

Simply scan the QR code below to leave your review:

Thank you for being a part of this community and for spreading the love. Your support means the world to me and to all the couples out there looking for a little help. Now, let's keep the game alive and make the world a more loving place, one relationship at a time.

- Your biggest fan, Riley

Chapter References

Chapter 1 References
1. PositivePsychology.com. (n.d.). *Active listening: The art of empathetic conversation*. https://positivepsychology.com/active-listening/
2. Flourish Psychology. (2023, February 14). *Gottman's 7 principles of making marriage work*. https://www.flourishpsychology.ca/post/gottmans-principles-of-making-marriage-work
3. Family Therapy Associates of Jacksonville. (2023, March 15). *How to conquer these 4 damaging communication barriers*. https://ftajax.com/4-damaging-communication-barriers/
4. Gonzalez, A. (2019). *The benefits of nonverbal immediacy behaviors to intimate relationships*. Journal of Undergraduate Research and Scholarly Works, 7. https://provost.utsa.edu/undergraduate-research/journal/files/vol7/JURSW.v7.09.Gonzalez.pdf

Chapter 2 References
5. Morin, A. (2023, January 12). *Healthy communication tips - relationships*. Verywell Mind. https://www.verywellmind.com/managing-conflict-in-relationships-communication-tips-3144967
6. Flourish Psychology. (2023, February 14). *Gottman's 7 principles of making marriage work*. https://www.flourishpsychology.ca/post/gottmans-principles-of-making-marriage-work
7. Firestone, L. (n.d.). *Preserving individuality to strengthen your relationship*. PsychAlive. https://www.psychalive.org/preserving-individuality-strengthen-relationship/
8. Gottman Institute. (2023, March 8). *Manage conflict: Repair and de-escalate*. https://www.gottman.com/blog/manage-conflict-repair-and-de-escalate/

Chapter 3 References
9. Morin, A. (2023, January 12). *Healthy communication tips - relationships*. Verywell Mind. https://www.verywellmind.com/managing-conflict-in-relationships-communication-tips-3144967
10. Sweet, E., Nandi, A., Adam, E. K., & McDade, T. W. (2021). *Long-term physical health consequences of financial stress*. Social Science & Medicine, 291, 114471. https://www.ncbi.nlm.nih.gov/pmc/articles/PMC8425299/
11. Gottman Institute. (n.d.). *Overview - Research*. https://www.gottman.com/about/research/.

12. Talkspace. (2023, February 17). *17 communication exercises for couples therapy*. https://www.talkspace.com/blog/communication-exercises-for-couples-therapy/

Chapter 4 References

13. Morin, A. (2023, January 12). *Healthy communication tips - relationships*. Verywell Mind. https://www.verywellmind.com/managing-conflict-in-relationships-communication-tips-3144967
14. San Diego Relationship Place. (2023, March 4). *7 Gottman-backed conflict resolution strategies in marriage*. https://www.sdrelationshipplace.com/conflict-resolution-strategies-in-marriage/
15. Healthy Minds NYC. (2023, January 23). *How to resolve financial stress in your relationship*. https://www.healthyminds.nyc/blog/how-to-resolve-financial-stress-in-your-relationship
16. McNulty, J. K. (2008). *Forgiveness in marriage: Putting the benefits into context*. Journal of Family Psychology, 22(2), 171-175. https://greatergood.berkeley.edu/images/uploads/McNulty-Longterm_Outcomes_of_Forgiveness_in_Marriage.pdf

Chapter 5 References

17. Calm. (2023, January 20). *How to build emotional connection in relationships*. Calm Blog. https://www.calm.com/blog/emotional-connection
18. Choosing Therapy. (2023, February 14). *12 marriage intimacy exercises for couples*. https://www.choosingtherapy.com/intimacy-exercises/
19. PsychCentral. (2023, March 11). *Vulnerability in relationships: Benefits and tips*. https://psychcentral.com/relationships/trust-and-vulnerability-in-relationships
20. PsychCentral. (2023, January 25). *6 steps to improving emotional intimacy with your partner*. https://psychcentral.com/blog/6-steps-to-improving-emotional-intimacy-with-your-partner

Chapter 6 References

21. DeLuca, S. (2022, July 12). *Why non-sexual touch is so essential*. Psychology Today. https://www.psychologytoday.com/us/blog/sexual-mindfulness/202207/why-non-sexual-touch-is-so-essential
22. Hughes, J. R., Waite, L. J., & Laumann, E. O. (2022). *Dimensions of couples' sexual communication and relationship satisfaction*. Archives of Sexual Behavior, 51(4), 1819-1834. https://www.ncbi.nlm.nih.gov/pmc/articles/PMC9153093/
23. Sprecher, S., & Treger, S. (2018). *Cross-cultural similarity in relationship-specific social support expectations*. Journal of Social and Personal Relationships, 35(5), 635-653. https://www.ncbi.nlm.nih.gov/pmc/articles/PMC6501924/

24. Gottman Institute. (2023, March 8). *Dr. Gottman's 3 skills (and 1 rule!) for intimate conversation*. https://www.gottman.com/blog/dr-gottmans-3-skills-and-1-rule-for-intimate-conversation/

Chapter 7 References

25. Bhandari, B. (2023, January 25). *One key to a happy marriage? A joint bank account*. Kellogg Insight. https://insight.kellogg.northwestern.edu/article/key-to-happy-marriage-joint-bank-account
26. LSS Financial Counseling. (2023, February 12). *How to work with your partner to reduce debt*. https://www.lssmn.org/financialcounseling/blog/debt-relationships/how-work-your-partner-reduce-debt
27. Danckwerts, S. E., & Leech, S. (2023, March 4). *The psychological impact of money on relationships*. Psychology Today. https://www.psychologytoday.com/us/blog/how-make-better-choices/202212/the-psychological-impact-money-relationships
28. Anspach, D. (2023, January 14). *How to create a budget with your spouse (in 7 steps)*. Investopedia. https://www.investopedia.com/articles/personal-finance/120315/how-create-budget-your-spouse.asp

Chapter 8 References

29. GovLoop. (2023, January 11). *4 ways to communicate during transition*. https://www.govloop.com/4-ways-to-communicate-during-transition/
30. Jansen, S. J. T., van Ham, M., & de Jong, T. (2023). *Firm relocations, commuting and relationship stability*. Regional Studies, Regional Science, 10(1), 25-41. https://www.tandfonline.com/doi/full/10.1080/21681376.2023.2174042
31. Los Angeles Times. (2022, November 1). *How to support a partner who's lost a loved one*. https://www.latimes.com/california/newsletter/2022-11-01/group-therapy-support-partner-grief-group-therapy
32. Lawrence, E., Rothman, A. D., Cobb, R. J., & Bradbury, T. N. (2008). *The effect of the transition to parenthood on relationship quality: An eight-year prospective study*. Journal of Personality and Social Psychology, 94(1), 208-223. https://www.ncbi.nlm.nih.gov/pmc/articles/PMC2702669/

Chapter 9 References

33. Morin, A. (2023, January 11). *Betrayal trauma: Causes, symptoms, impact, and coping*. Verywell Mind. https://www.verywellmind.com/betrayal-trauma-causes-symptoms-impact-and-coping-5270361
34. Gottman Institute. (2023, March 8). *How to build trust with your partner after infidelity*. https://www.gottman.com/blog/how-to-build-trust-with-your-partner-after-infidelity/
35. Labuzan Lopez, E. (2024, January 17). *The role of empathy in relationship repair*. https://www.erikalabuzanlopeztherapy.com/blog-psychotherapy-

marriage-counseling-infertility-postpartum-depression-minimalism-leaguecity-houston-tx/2024/1/17/the-role-of-empathy-in-relationship-repair

36. Dym, R. (2024, January 5). *Healing after infidelity: The role of therapy for affairs in relationship recovery*. LinkedIn. https://www.linkedin.com/pulse/healing-after-infidelity-role-therapy-affairs-dymre.

Chapter 10 References

37. Fox, J. (2014, October 1). *What's really behind jealousy, and what to do about it*. Psychology Today. https://www.psychologytoday.com/us/blog/close-encounters/201410/whats-really-behind-jealousy-and-what-do-about-it

38. Navarro, C. (2016, May 3). *10 steps to effective couples communication*. Psychology Today. https://www.psychologytoday.com/us/blog/lifetime-connections/201605/10-steps-to-effective-couples-communication

39. PositivePsychology.com. (n.d.). *18 best self-esteem worksheets and activities (incl. PDF)*. https://positivepsychology.com/self-esteem-worksheets/

40. Pew Research Center. (2020, May 8). *Dating and relationships in the digital age*. https://www.pewresearch.org/internet/2020/05/08/dating-and-relationships-in-the-digital-age/

Chapter 11 References

41. Bradbury, T. N., & Karney, B. R. (2004). *The role of appreciation in relationships: A journal study*. Journal of Marriage and Family, 66(3), 646-658. https://diginole.lib.fsu.edu/islandora/object/fsu:181628/datastream/PDF/view

42. Gottman Institute. (2023, January 20). *3 research-based tips for a happy and healthy relationship*. https://www.gottman.com/blog/3-research-based-tips-for-a-happy-and-healthy-relationship/

43. HelpGuide. (n.d.). *Setting healthy boundaries in relationships*. https://www.helpguide.org/articles/relationships-communication/setting-healthy-boundaries-in-relationships.htm

44. Williamsburg Therapy Group. (2023, February 10). *10+ effective communication exercises for couples*. https://williamsburgtherapygroup.com/blog/10-effective-communication-exercises-for-couples

Chapter 12 References

45. Morin, A. (2023, January 12). *Healthy communication tips - relationships*. Verywell Mind. https://www.verywellmind.com/managing-conflict-in-relationships-communication-tips-3144967

46. HelloPrenup. (2023, February 14). *Balancing individual and couple goals in a marriage*. https://helloprenup.com/relationships/balancing-individual-and-couple-goals-in-a-marriage/

47. Gottman Institute. (2023, March 8). *Manage conflict: The art of compromise*. https://www.gottman.com/blog/manage-conflict-the-art-of-compromise/

48. Adventure Book. (2023, March 1). *Relationship milestones worth remembering*. https://www.adventurebook.com/connect/relationship-milestones/

Printed in Great Britain
by Amazon